The Effect of Changes in Regulatory Capital Requirements on Bank Lending

Berenger Piper

The Effect of Changes in Regulatory Capital Requirements on Bank Lending

A Case Study of Canadian Banks

palgrave
macmillan

Berenger Piper
Business Science Institute & Macro Insight Research Hub
Luxembourg City & Toronto, Luxembourg & Canada

ISBN 978-3-032-02207-3 ISBN 978-3-032-02208-0 (eBook)
https://doi.org/10.1007/978-3-032-02208-0

This Palgrave Macmillan imprint is published by the registered company Springer Nature Switzerland AG.
The registered company address is: Gewerbestrasse 11, 6330 Cham, Switzerland.

About the Author

Berenger Piper is a financial economist based in Toronto, Canada, with nearly 15 years of experience in financial risk management. He is currently an associate director in the Capital Market Risks and Controls Division of one of the Top 3 Canadian Investment Banks in Toronto.

He holds a doctorate of business administration in financial economics from Jean Moulin University Lyon 3 (IAE Lyon School of Management), France, and The Business Science Institute, Luxembourg.

In addition to his professional achievements in the banking sector, Piper is a researcher in financial economics, with research interests in macroprudential and microprudential regulations, financial markets, financial stability, asset pricing, and risk management.

Acknowledgements

This book presents a study on the impact of the variations of regulatory bank capital requirements on the lending behaviour of Canadian banks. Our results provided further clarity to the existing and scarce literature on this topic. The research also provided Canadian regulators and policymakers with guidelines and conditions necessary for the increase of the level of regulatory bank capital requirements. This work would not have been possible without the support of various individuals and institutions.

Firstly, I would like to thank my family, specifically my wife (Keinza Piper) and my son (Milian Piper), for their sacrifice and support throughout the process that led to this book.

Secondly, I am particularly grateful to Professor Laurent Weill (EM Strasbourg Business School, France) for his unwavering support, guidance, and encouragement.

Thirdly, I would like to express my gratitude to Professor Michel Kalika (Business Science Institute, Luxembourg) and Professor Nathalie Mitev (Business Science Institute, Luxembourg) for their feedback, guidance, and support.

Finally, I am very thankful for the assistance and support received from the Business Science Institute's academic support team (Catherine Rousseaux, Yasemin Ozuag, Stephen Platt, Frédéric Branger), just to name a few. This book project would not have been successful without their assistance and guidance.

Contents

CHAPTER 1

General Introduction

Abstract This book studied the impact of a microprudential and macroprudential regulation on the lending behaviour of financial institutions. Specifically, the research studied the impact of changes in regulatory capital requirements on the lending behaviour of Canadian banks.

The general introduction presents an overview of regulatory capital requirements and financial soundness indicators, an evolution of Basel Accords, and a summary of capital requirements rules set by the Office of the Superintendent of Financial Institutions (OSFI). The general introduction also provides details on the structure of the remaining sections of the book.

Keywords Basel Accords • Regulatory Capital Requirements • Canadian Bank Lending Behaviour • Macroprudential Regulations • Microprudential Regulations • Financial Soundness Indicators • Countercyclical Buffer • Capital Conservation Buffer • Domestic Stability Buffer • Gross Domestic Product (GDP) • Bank for International Settlements (BIS) • World Bank

The subprime crisis of 2008 revealed the limits of the financial system in place before the crisis and opened the door for further enhancements to the microeconomic and macroeconomic policies in place to ensure

B. Piper, *The Effect of Changes in Regulatory Capital Requirements on Banks Lending*
https://doi.org/10.1007/978-3-032-02208-0_1

financial stability. The crisis demonstrated the serious lack of sufficient capital reserves in financial institutions, particularly in banks. The lack of sufficient capital reserves led to a review of the Basel I and II Accords. Hence, the Basel Committee on Banking Supervision designed and imposed on banks the implementation of Basel III (Third Basel Accord) to reinforce the level and quality of capital reserves required by banks.

Regulatory capital requirements have been used by national financial regulators as a fundamental instrument to set and monitor the level of capital reserves required to be set aside by banks to ensure their resilience in times of financial distress. The capital requirements are therefore regulatory mechanism aimed at fostering financial stability. While regulatory capital requirements represent an important microeconomic and macroeconomic policy tool, it is important to investigate how they impact the determinants of the level of liquidity made available by banks to finance the non-financial corporate sector.

The determinants of the level of liquidity made available by banks to finance the non-financial corporate sector are mainly the volume of gross loans that banks are likely to lend to the non-financial sector following increases in regulatory capital requirements, the level of interest rates that banks are willing to charge for their lending facilities to the non-financial sector, and the impact that changes in regulatory capital requirements have on the gross loan portfolio of banks.

In the context of the Canadian financial sector, the portfolio of gross loans to the non-financial sector is compound of mainly corporate loans, mortgage and residential loans, and retail and consumer loans. Bank interest rates represent the bank interest income obtained by Canadian banks from loans offered to the non-financial sector.

Regulatory capital requirements were designed to ensure that banks withstand liquidity shocks in time of economic uncertainty. Banks in major global economies have gone through periods of instability and failure during the period ranging between 1950 and the 1980s. Particularly, banks in the USA have been impacted by approximately six bank bankruptcies between 1950 and 1981.[1] The rhythm of occurrence of bank failures or bankruptcies in the USA became very severe in the 1980s. The severity of the bank failures in the 1980s made economists and financial experts characterised the period of the 1980s as the era of savings and loan

[1] Federal Reserve Bank of St. Louis, Coping with Bank Failures: Some Lessons from the United States and the United Kingdom. Available from https://files.stlouisfed.org/files/htdocs/publications/review/86/12/Coping_Dec1986.pdf. August 2023.

crisis. This period of distress lasted till 1989 and impacted primarily the savings and loan industry.[2]

The era of savings and loan crisis was preceded by the bank failures of the 1970s that led to high inflation and interest rates. This caused savers to withdraw their funds due to the disparities between the interest rate charged for loans and the interest rates that savers could earn on their deposits. The interest rate that banks could pay to savers on their deposits was set by the federal government in the USA and was significantly low in comparison to the interest value that savers could earn if they were to place their deposits in other markets. Additionally, the terms of the mortgage products offered during the era of savings and loan crisis had long amortisation terms. The rise of inflation and interest rates during that period negatively impacted the value of these mortgage products. The loss of value of these mortgage products increased the severity of the bank failures in the 1980s.

The negative and contagion effects of the bank failures in the USA and other major economies led to the creation of the Basel Committee on Banking Supervision to prevent and mitigate future bank failure risks. The Basel Committee on Banking Supervision, initially made of central bankers and supervisory authorities from a group of ten countries (G10) agreed on the need to establish multinational capital requirements to strengthen the stability of the international banking system. The agreement on the need to harmonise bank capital requirements across the global economy, resulted in the adoption of the Basel Capital Accord (Capital Measurement System) by the G10 governors and its communication in 1988.[3] The Basel Capital Accord released in 1988 documented the first Basel rule, also known as the Basel I Capital Accord, which sets the minimum risk-based capital adequacy ratio that banks are required to maintain. The Basel I Capital Accord was enhanced to further strengthen the financial stability of the global economy. These enhancements were documented in the Basel II and Basel III Capital Accords.

The Basel I Capital Accord focused mainly on strengthening the stability of the global banking system; and reducing competitive differences and inequalities amongst financial institutions globally. The Basel I Capital Accord achieved these objectives by setting a minimum capital adequacy

[2] Federal Reserve History, Savings and Loan Crisis. Available from https://www.federalreservehistory.org/essays/savings-and-loan-crisis. August 2023.

[3] The Bank for International Settlements, History of the Basel Committee. Available from https://www.bis.org/bcbs/history.htm. August 2023.

ratio that is applicable to all banks internationally. This represented a major achievement and closed a gap that remained opened till the adoption of the Basel I Capital Accord. The global banking system did not have a harmonised minimum capital requirement, prior to the adoption of the Basel I Capital Accord.

The Basel I Capital Accord classified bank capital into two tiers. The first tier of capital known as Tier 1 encompasses the core capital of the bank. The core capital of banks is made of shareholder equity and declared reserves.

The second tier of capital known as Tier 2 covers additional capital derived from gains made from the investments of assets, interests from long-term debts with maturity levels higher than 5 years, and other reserves.[4]

Despite achieving its main purpose, the Basel I Capital Accord had several limitations that required enhancements of the initial rules.

The first limitation of the Basel I Capital Accord is its static evaluation of banks' default risk. The Basel I Capital Accord does not consider the possibility that banks' default risk may change over time. The possible change in banks' default risk indicates that the capital adequacy ratio of 8% may not always be sufficient to ensure that banks withstand potential effects of periods of economic distress.

The second limitation of the Basel I Capital Accord is that it does not consider the different aspects of credit risk. The accord is impacted by its limited approach to credit risk differentiation.

The third limitation of the Basel I Capital Accord resides in the fact that it does not consider the heterogeneity of currencies financial markets and banking systems, globally. The rule does not consider the differences in currency and macroeconomic risks globally. This led to an inaccurate estimation of potential counterparty risk.

The fourth limitation of the Basel I Capital Accord is that it ignores the negative impacts of non-diversification of bank portfolios.

The fifth limitation of the Basel I Capital Accord is that the minimum capital requirement set does not consider the maturity of credit exposure. The capital requirement rule under the Basel I Capital Accord remains static regardless of the term-structure of banks' credit risk or exposure.

The five limitations of the Basel I Capital Accord led to the design and adoption of the Basel II Capital Accord.

The Basel Committee on Banking Supervision adopted the Basel II Capital Accord in 2004. The Basel II Capital Accord enhanced the Basel I

[4] Bank for International Settlements, International Convergence of Capital Measurement and Capital Standards. Available from https://www.bis.org/publ/bcbs04a.pdf. August 2023.

Capital Accord by introducing more stringent regulatory capital requirements, a thorough supervisory review process, and mandatory market disclosures. The stringent regulatory capital requirements, supervisory review process, and mandatory market disclosures represent the main pillars of the Basel II Capital Accord.

Contrarily to the Basel I Capital Accord where the eligible regulatory capital of the banks is divided into two tiers, the Basel II Capital Accord[5] divides the eligible regulatory capital of the banks into three tiers.

The first tier under the Basel II Capital Accord covers banks' core capital also known as common stocks, disclosed reserves, and other assets. The capital requirement under the Basel II Capital Accord is more stringent. The Basel II Capital Accord requires that a minimum of 4% of banks' capital reserves must derive from the bank's core capital.

The second tier under the Basel II Capital Accord covers additional capital emanating from other reserves, hybrid instruments, medium or long-term subordinated loans.

The third tier under the Basel II Capital Accord encompasses unsecured and subordinated debt. The components of the third tier are considered to be of the lowest quality.

The components of the first and second tiers under the Basel II Capital Accord have the highest and medium levels of quality, respectively. The components of the first tier under the Basel II Capital Accord are considered to be made of more secure and liquid assets in comparison to the second and third tiers.

The Basel II Capital Accord introduced the notion of risk-weighted assets (RWAs),[6] with the aim of controlling the level of risk banks are allowed to take through assets that they acquire. The Basel II Capital Accord obliged banks to factor the credit rating of the assets that they hold into their risk weights estimations. The inclusion of the credit rating of assets held by banks into their weighted risk estimation means that banks holding assets with good credit ratings would have lower risk weights.

The Basel II Capital Accord designed and implemented a supervision framework that supports national supervisory bodies to address legal,

[5] Bank for International Settlements, Basel II: International Convergence of Capital Measurement and Capital Standards. Available from https://www.bis.org/publ/bcbs118.pdf. August 2023.

[6] Bank for International Settlements, Basel II: International Convergence of Capital Measurement and Capital Standards. Available from https://www.bis.org/publ/bcbs118.pdf. August 2023.

systemic, and liquidity risks. The supervision framework designed by the Basel II Capital Accord enables enhanced regulatory supervision, which contributes to the soundness and stability of the international banking system.

The supervision framework under the Basel II Capital Accord is supported by the market discipline pillar which introduced mandatory market disclosures reporting on banks' risk assessment processes, capital adequacy, and risk exposures. The introduction of mandatory market disclosures enabled fairness and transparency on market risk and banks' exposures.

Although the Basel II Capital Accord enhanced the Basel I Capital Accord, its limits[7] were revealed through the subprime crisis of 2008. The Basel II Capital Accord falls short[8] from considering the internal practices within banks and the risk inherent to these internal bank practices, as well as the undercapitalisation of banks globally. The undercapitalisation of banks internationally that was revealed through the subprime crisis of 2008 was partially missed by prudential regulators due to the lack of liquidity ratios to detect banks with inadequate leverage and liquidity buffers.

The failure of the Lehman Brothers in September 2008 confirmed the need to urgently review the limitations of the Basel II Capital Accord and design a new Basel Capital Accord that addresses the limitations of the Basel II Capital Accord. The Basel Committee responded[9] to the urgent reforms to the Basel II Capital Accord by issuing risk management and supervision guidelines to address the immediate consequences of the subprime crisis of 2008 on the banking system and global financial system. Following the post-crisis immediate reforms, the Basel Committee initiated the design of the Basel III Capital Accord to thoroughly address the limitations of the Basel III Capital Accord.

The Basel III Capital Accord was designed after the subprime crisis of 2008 to address the limitations of the Basel II Capital Accord. The Basel III Capital Accord proposed a set of leverage ratios and level of capital reserves to address the gaps exposed by the financial crisis of 2008. The Basel III Capital Accord built on the foundations of the Basel I and Basel II Capital Accords, with the aim of mitigating systemic risk with the financial sector, by strengthening the ability of each bank to remain resilient

[7] Bank for International Settlements, Basel III: Responding to the 2007-09 Financial Crisis. Available from https://www.bis.org/bcbs/history.htm. August 2023.

[8] Bank for International Settlements. Basel III: responding to the 2007-09 financial crisis. Available from https://www.bis.org/bcbs/history.htm. August 2023.

[9] Bank for International Settlements. Basel III: responding to the 2007-09 financial crisis. Available from https://www.bis.org/bcbs/history.htm. August 2023.

during times of economic and financial distresses. The Basel III Capital Accord took effect on 1 January 2023.

The Basel III Capital Accord proposed two tiers for the classification of banks' capital. The first tier of the Basel III Capital Accord encompasses banks' capital, shareholders' equity, and disclosed reserves.

The second tier of the Basel III Capital Accord covers additional capital made of unsecured subordinated debt instruments, and other (undisclosed) reserves. The Basel III Capital Accord recommends that banks maintain a minimum capital adequacy ratio of 8% of RWAs, including a Tier 1 capital adequacy ratio of at least 6%.[10] The Basel III Capital Accord set the minimum of capital ratio from Tier 1 to 6%, representing an increase of 2% (from 4% to 6%) in comparison to the Basel II Capital Accord. The Basel III Capital Accord removed the inclusion of a third tier (Tier 3)[11] from the estimation of regulatory capital requirements.

In addition to strengthening the Tier 1 and Tier 2 components of the total capital ratio, the Basel III Capital Accord recommends additional capital buffers[12] amounting from 0 to 2.5% of banks' RWAs, which are required to derive from the Tier 1 components of banks' capital. The additional capital buffers, commonly referred to as the countercyclical capital buffers are required from banks to ensure that they are not undercapitalised during times of economic crisis or financial distresses. The application of countercyclical capital buffer requirements means that under the Basel III Capital Accord, banks are required to maintain a minimum total capital requirement of 10.5%.[13]

The Basel III Capital Accord introduced leverage and liquidity ratio requirements to control for risks derived from excessive lending activities, which could lead to banks becoming undercapitalised. Hence, the Basel III Accord required that global systemically important banks maintain a leverage ratio of at least 3%.[14] The leverage ratio for global systemically

[10] Bank for International Settlements, Minimum Risk-Based Capital Requirements. Available from https://www.bis.org/basel_framework/chapter/RBC/20.htm. August 2023.

[11] Bank for International Settlements, Minimum Risk-Based Capital Requirements. Available from https://www.bis.org/basel_framework/chapter/RBC/20.htm. August 2023.

[12] Bank for International Settlements, Minimum Risk-Based Capital Requirements. Available from https://www.bis.org/basel_framework/chapter/RBC/20.htm. August 2023.

[13] Bank for International Settlements, The Capital Buffers in Basel III – Executive Summary. Available from https://www.bis.org/fsi/fsisummaries/b3_capital.htm. August 2023.

[14] Bank for International Settlements, The Capital Buffers in Basel III – Executive Summary. Available from https://www.bis.org/fsi/fsisummaries/b3_capital.htm. August 2023.

important banks under the Basel III Accord is calculated through estimation of the ratio of the Tier 1 component of banks' capital over bank's total (aggregated) assets.

The Basel III Capital Accord also recommends a minimum liquidity coverage ratio (LCR) of 100% requiring that banks hold sufficient reserves of funds derived from High Quality Liquid Assets (HQLA) to withstand periods of financial stress that last up to 30 days. HQLA encompass assets that are highly liquid, and which can be converted into liquid or cash, without deterioration of their values.[15]

The net stable funding (NSF) ratio also represents an additional prudential buffer recommended by the Basel III Capital Accord. The NSF ratio must be 100% at minimum and its aim is to help banks build secure funding and reserves over the long term, rather than accumulating short term debts.[16]

Table 1.1 summarises the requirements of the Basel I, Basel II, and Basel III Capital Accords.

Table 1.1 Summary of requirements of Basel I, Basel II, and Basel III Capital Accords

Basel Requirements	*Basel I Capital Accord*	*Basel II Capital Accord*	*Basel III Capital Accord*
Ratio of Capital Conservation Buffer to RWAs	N/A	N/A	0–2.5%
Ratio of Minimum Capital Adequacy to RWAs	8%	8%	10.5%
Ratio of Minimum Common Equity to RWAs	N/A	2%	4.5%
Ratio of Tier 1 Capital to RWAs	N/A	4%	6%
Minimum Leverage Ratio	N/A	N/A	3%
Minimum Liquidity Coverage Ratio	N/A	N/A	100%
NSF Ratio	N/A	N/A	100%

Source: Designed on the basis of the information presented on Basel I, II, and III Capital Accords in previous paragraphs.

[15] Bank for International Settlements, The Capital Buffers in Basel III – Executive Summary. Available from https://www.bis.org/fsi/fsisummaries/b3_capital.htm. August 2023.

[16] Bank for International Settlements, The Capital Buffers in Basel III – Executive Summary. Available from https://www.bis.org/fsi/fsisummaries/b3_capital.htm. August 2023.

The Basel Capital Accords were reinforced by the Financial Stability Board (FSB) through the Total Loss-Absorbing Capacity (TLAC)[17] agreement on the adequacy of TLAC for Global Systemically Important Banks (G-SIBs). The TLAC was agreed following consultations between the Basel Committee and the FSB. The TLAC sets standards of principles that require the permanent provision of sufficient loss-absorbing and recapitalisation capacity to avoid negative impacts to financial stability, use of public funds, and inability to continue with critical functions in the event of a resolution.

The Minimum Requirement for Own Funds and Eligible Liabilities (MREL)[18] are also additional requirements set by resolution authorities to ensure that banks permanently maintain sufficient eligible instruments to facilitate the implementation of the preferred resolution strategy.

The subsections 485(1) and 949(1) of the Bank Act (BA),[19] subsection 473(1) of the Trust and Loan Companies Act (TLCA) mandate Canadian banks, Canadian credit unions, Canadian bank holding companies, and Canadian federally regulated loan companies to maintain a minimum capital adequacy ratio.

The Office of the Superintendent of Financial Institutions (OSFI)[20] is the Canadian regulator of financial institutions. OSFI acts as an independent federal government agency that regulates and supervises more than 400 federally regulated financial institutions (FRFIs) in Canada.

The regulation role of OSFI is carried out through the developments of rules, guidelines, and the interpretation of legislation and regulations. OSFI's supervision role includes economic analysis, analysis of financial trends, and identification of emerging issues requiring new rules, standards, guidelines, and further supervision.

[17] Financial Stability Board (FSB), Principles on Loss-Absorbing and Recapitalisation Capacity of G-SIBs in Resolution. Available from https://www.fsb.org/wp-content/uploads/TLAC-Principles-and-Term-Sheet-for-publication-final.pdf. August 2023.

[18] Single Resolution Board, The Minimum Requirement for Own Funds and Eligible Liabilities (MREL). Available from https://www.srb.europa.eu/en/system/files?file=media/document/mrel_policy_may_2021_final_web.pdf#:~:text=The%20minimum%20requirement%20for%20own%20funds%20and%20eligible,facilitate%20the%20implementation%20of%20the%20preferred%20resolution%20strategy. August 2023.

[19] Office of the Superintendent of Financial Institutions (OSFI), Capital Adequacy Requirements (CAR) Chapter 1 – Overview. Available from https://www.osfi-bsif.gc.ca/en/guidance/guidance-library/capital-adequacy-requirements-car-2024-chapter-1-overview-risk-based-capital-requirements. August 2023.

[20] Office of the Superintendent of Financial Institutions (OSFI), Our Role. Available from https://www.osfi-bsif.gc.ca/Eng/osfi-bsif/Pages/default.aspx. August 2023.

The OSFI is a member of the Basel Committee on Banking Supervision. The minimum risk-based capital and leverage ratios required by OSFI were established following the guidelines of the Basel Committee. Canadian capital adequacy and leverage requirements are applicable to Canadian financial institutions designated by OSFI as Domestic Systemically Important Banks (D-SIBs) and Small and Medium-Sized Banks (SMSBs).[21] OSFI defines RWAs as the highest value of the sum of RWA for credit risk, RWA for market risk, and RWA for operational risk.[22]

In addition to a minimum capital requirement set at 8% of RWAs, OSFI also requires D-SIBs and SMSBs to maintain the following key mandatory capital buffers[23]:

- Levels of **Capital Adequacy Ratios** during periods of economic upswings that are higher than the minimum capital requirement. The OSFI minimum capital requirement is set at 8% of RWAs.
- In addition to the minimum capital requirements, a **Capital Conservation Buffer (CCB)** of 2.5% of RWAs, calculated using only Common Equity Tier 1 capital (CET1) is required. This translates into 10.5% of RWAs.
- A **Countercyclical Buffer** is set by OSFI to consider the Canadian macroeconomic and financial environment. Financial institutions can be subject to a countercyclical buffer of up to 2.5% of RWAs.
- Designated financial institutions are required to maintain **D-SIB Surcharge**. The Bank of Montreal, Bank of Nova Scotia, Canadian Imperial Bank of Commerce, National Bank of Canada, Royal Bank of Canada, and Toronto-Dominion Bank have been designated by OSFI as D-SIBs and are required to maintain a CET1 surcharge of 1% of RWAs.
- A **Domestic Stability Buffer (DSB)** of up to 2.5% of D-SIBs' RWAs is required. The DSB was established by OSFI to cover any vulnerabilities contained in the aforementioned capital requirements.

[21] Office of the Superintendent of Financial Institutions, Overview of Risk-Based Capital Requirements – Scope of Application. Available from https://www.osfi-bsif.gc.ca/Eng/fi-if/rg-ro/gdn-ort/gl-ld/Pages/CAR22_chpt1.aspx. July 2022.

[22] Office of the Superintendent of Financial Institutions, Overview of Risk-Based Capital Requirements – Total Risk-Weighted Assets. Available from https://www.osfi-bsif.gc.ca/Eng/fi-if/rg-ro/gdn-ort/gl-ld/Pages/CAR22_chpt1.aspx. July 2022.

[23] Office of the Superintendent of Financial Institutions, Overview of Risk-Based Capital Requirements – Mandated Capital Buffers. Available from https://www.osfi-bsif.gc.ca/Eng/fi-if/rg-ro/gdn-ort/gl-ld/Pages/CAR22_chpt1.aspx. July 2022.

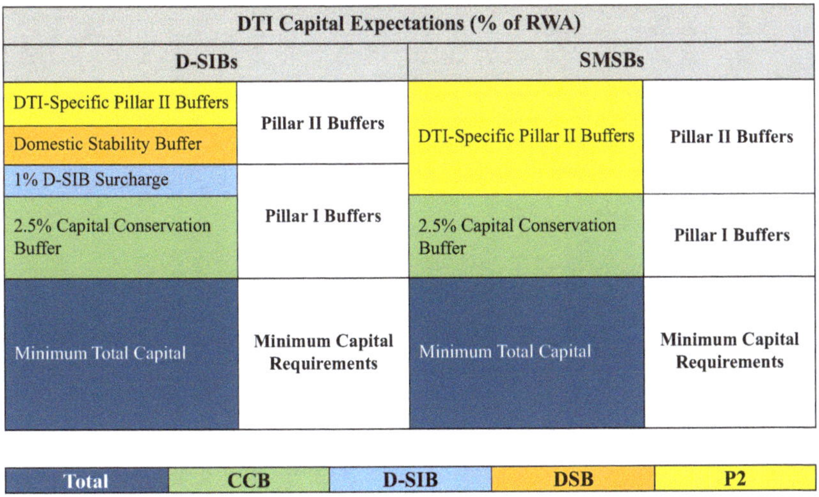

Fig. 1.1 OSFI capital requirements in percentage of RWAs from DTIs (Source: Office of the Superintendent of Financial Institutions, *Overview of Risk-Based Capital Requirements – Annex 2 Supervisory Target Capital Requirements.* Available from https://www.osfi-bsif.gc.ca/Eng/fi-if/rg-ro/gdn-ort/gl-ld/Pages/CAR22_chpt1.aspx, July 2022).

Figure 1.1 summarises and illustrates OSFI capital requirements in percentage of RWAs from Deposit-Taking Institutions (DTIs).

Financial Soundness Indicators are prudential indicators utilised to measure the financial soundness and stability of a financial system. Financial Soundness Indicators (FSIs) include capital adequacy ratio, as well as efficiency, liquidity, and profitability ratios. The International Monetary Fund (IMF) compiles the statistics of FSIs on financial systems globally.

Table 1.2 presents the FSIs[24] on the financial systems of Canada, the USA, Australia, and advanced European economies.

The FSIs on financial systems (Canada, the USA, Australia, and advanced European economies) presented in Table 1.2 are based on the Capital Adequacy Ratio (Regulatory Capital to RWAs percentage) maintained by the financial system of each of the advanced economies between 2010 and 2022.

[24] The International Monetary Fund (IMF), Financial Soundness Indicators (FSIs). Available from https://data.imf.org/regular.aspx?key=63174546. August 2023.

Table 1.2 FSIs on financial systems (Canada, USA, Australia, and advanced European economies) (capital adequacy, regulatory capital to RWAs, percentage)

Advanced Economies	*2010*	*2011*	*2012*	*2013*	*2014*	*2015*	*2016*	*2017*	*2018*	*2019*	*2020*	*2021*	*2022*
Australia	11.40	11.58	11.92	11.61	12.22	13.80	13.70	14.61	14.80	15.70	17.56	17.87	17.80
Austria	15.44	15.83	16.96	17.97	16.25	16.54	17.98	18.84	18.36	18.35	19.16	18.48	
Belgium	19.30	18.54	18.19	18.74	17.58	18.69	18.81	18.96	18.76	18.75	20.34	20.44	20.05
Canada	15.57	15.89	16.16	14.33	14.23	14.20	14.76	14.81	15.25	15.34	16.10	17.13	17.32
Cyprus	12.41	12.12	7.34	14.03	15.36	16.47	16.79	16.29	17.32	19.55	20.27	20.65	21.21
Czech Rep.	15.27	14.97	15.62	16.52	16.98	17.57	17.66	18.07	18.29	19.69	22.11	21.19	20.27
Denmark	16.01	17.19	18.88	19.24	18.21	19.19	20.75	22.15	21.68	22.47	23.29	22.87	22.56
Estonia, Rep. of	22.07	18.61	19.32	19.97	35.65	36.53	35.09	30.61	31.01	27.03	27.89	24.37	21.98
Finland	14.41	14.19	16.98	15.98	17.29	22.91	23.34	21.42	21.53	20.50	20.56	20.59	20.33
France	12.67	12.32	14.50	15.38	15.20	16.40	17.74	17.90	18.04	18.85	19.53	19.73	19.10
Germany	16.05	16.40	17.94	19.16	17.96	18.26	18.79	19.38	18.90	18.58	19.19	18.83	18.50
Greece	12.26	–1.67	9.57	13.51	14.07	16.52	16.95	17.02	15.99	17.02	16.66	15.23	17.46
Iceland					28.55	28.22	27.66	25.05	23.18	24.17	24.92	25.39	23.70
Ireland	14.47	18.92	19.24	21.17	22.68	27.49	27.31	25.34	25.39	24.97	25.47	25.53	24.57
Italy	12.07	12.68	13.42	13.70	14.30	14.79	13.75	16.71	16.05	17.16	19.29	18.81	19.18
Latvia	13.91	16.53	16.74	18.05	19.68	21.82	20.38	20.82	22.31	21.69	26.82	25.34	23.03
Luxembourg	17.38	16.35	19.05	20.88	20.24	22.04	24.65	25.91	25.00	21.91	24.32	23.92	22.76
Malta	14.80	15.48	16.08	16.51	14.73	15.00	16.16	17.28	18.13	20.08	21.66	22.68	23.01
Netherlands, The	13.91	13.48	14.23	14.89	17.95	20.11	22.38	22.03	22.30	22.87	22.82	22.37	20.97
Norway	14.19	13.59	14.57	15.52	16.49	18.94	22.07	22.02	22.33	24.19	24.80	25.02	23.72
Portugal	10.33	9.78	12.64	13.31	12.25	13.33	12.27	15.15	15.15	16.93	17.97	18.01	17.54
Slovak Rep.	11.58	13.41	15.71	17.23	17.35	17.77	18.04	18.56	18.27	18.16	19.67	19.81	19.61
Slovenia, Rep. of	11.32	11.85	11.40	13.67	17.99	18.77	19.15	18.18	17.95	18.54	18.29	18.23	18.54
Spain	11.87	12.11	11.59	13.28	13.68	14.66	14.85	15.55	15.58	15.91	16.98	17.43	16.68
Sweden	12.00	11.48	11.74	11.96	22.50	24.22	26.88	26.38	21.58	22.78	23.49	22.96	22.69
Switzerland	17.06	16.59	16.87	18.66	16.61	17.02	16.08	18.57	18.62	19.33	19.69	19.57	19.07
The UK	15.89	15.73	17.07	19.61	17.32	19.61	20.64	20.69	21.39	21.25	21.61	22.05	21.36
The USA	14.79	14.69	14.51	14.41	14.39	14.14	14.19	14.53	14.77	14.65	16.28	16.39	15.54

The FSIs presented in Table 1.2 also show that regulatory capital ratios maintained by Canadian banks fluctuated around 16% between 2010 and 2012, decreased to approximately 14% between 2013 and 2017, and increased from 15.25% to 17.32% between 2018 and 2022.

The period of 2010 to 2012 represents the immediate post-economic crisis period after the subprime crisis of 2008, and the period ranging from 2013 to 2017 is characterised by the global economic recovery time after the subprime crisis of 2008.

The increase from 15.25% to 17.32% between 2018 and 2022 is not surprising and explains the transition to Basel III.

The data (Table 1.2) shows significant differences in the Capital Adequacy Ratio maintained in each of these advanced economies for each year. For example, the Capital Adequacy Ratios maintained by financial systems in Belgium, Denmark, Estonia, Finland, Germany, Iceland, Ireland, Luxembourg, Norway, Sweden, and Switzerland, during most of the period ranging from 2010 to 2022, are higher than those maintained by Canadian financial institutions over the same period.

Similarly, the data (Table 1.2) shows that, for example, the Capital Adequacy Ratios maintained by financial systems in Australia, Spain, and the USA, during most of the period ranging from 2010 to 2022, are lower than those maintained by Canadian financial institutions over the same period.

The differences noted in the FSIs on financial systems in Australia, advanced European economies, and the USA in comparison to the Canadian FSIs raised the question as to whether banks in each of these economies would have similar lending behaviour when subject to increases in regulatory capital requirements. The current literature on regulatory capital requirements has limited single-country studies, and there are practically no studies on the impact of regulatory capital requirements on the behaviour of Canadian banks.

Furthermore, the Canadian economy is one of the top largest world's economies and plays a significant role in the global financial system. The size of the Canadian economy further explains the importance of the study of the impact of regulatory capital requirements on the behaviour of Canadian banks.

Table 1.3 presents the Gross Domestic Product (GDP) in US currency for the Top 10 world's economies in 2022.

The country GDP data presented in Table 1.3 indicates that as of 2022, Canada was positioned as the 9th largest world's economy.

Table 1.3 GDP in US currency for the top 10 world's economies in 2022

Country	*Most Recent Year*	*Most Recent Value (Million USD)*
The USA	2022	25,462,700.00
China	2022	17,963,170.52
Japan	2022	4,231,141.20
Germany	2022	4,072,191.74
India	2022	3,385,089.88
The UK	2022	3,070,667.73
France	2022	2,782,905.33
Russian Federation	2022	2,240,422.44
Canada	2022	2,139,840.02
Italy	2022	2,010,431.60

Source: The World Bank, GDP (current US$) – Canada. Available from https://data.worldbank.org/indicator/NY.GDP.MKTP.CD?locations=CA&most_recent_value_desc=true. August 2023.

Therefore, the following points outline the need for a study on the impact of regulatory capital requirements on the behaviour of banks, within the Canadian context:

- Significant differences in the FSIs on financial systems of the American, Australian, Canadian, and advanced European economies.
- The differences in FSIs may mean that banks in different economies would have different lending behaviour when subject to increases in regulatory capital requirements.
- The size of the Canadian economy as the 9th top world's economy as of 2022, further justifies the importance of the study of the impact of regulatory capital requirements on the behaviour of Canadian banks.
- The current literature on regulatory capital requirements has limited single-country studies.
- There are practically no studies on the impact of regulatory capital requirements on the behaviour of Canadian banks.
- The study of the impact of regulatory capital requirements on the behaviour of Canadian banks will make contributions to the literature and provide regulators and policymakers with further policy guidance.

In addition to the general introduction and conclusion chapters, this book presents three empirical chapters which discuss the impact of changes in regulatory capital requirements on the lending behaviour of Canadian banks.

Empirical Chapter 2 of this book presents an empirical study that investigates the impact of banks' regulatory capital requirements on the lending volume of Canadian banks.

Empirical Chapter 3 of this book presents an empirical that analyses the effect of banks' regulatory capital requirements on the level of loan interest rates charged by Canadian banks for their loans to the non-financial sector.

Empirical Chapter 4 of this book presents an empirical that tested the impact of regulatory capital requirements on the gross loan portfolio of Canadian banks.

The three empirical studies presented of this book are linked by the components of lending facilities offered by banks. Each of the three empirical studies of this book study the impact of regulatory capital requirements on at least one of the components of the lending facilities offered by banks.

A general conclusion will summarise the conclusions derived from the results of the three empirical studies and highlight the policy recommendations that emanated from the results.

CHAPTER 2

Impact of Bank Regulatory Capital Requirements: On Canadian Banks' Gross Lending Volume

Abstract This chapter investigated the impact of changes in regulatory capital requirements on the volume of gross loans offered by Canadian banks to the non-financial sector, using econometric methodologies.

The study used a sample of annual financial statistics of Canadian financial institutions from 2012 to 2021, from Fitch Connect database, over the period of 2012 to 2021. The data also encompasses macroeconomic statistics from the Bank of Canada, BIS, and Economic Policy Uncertainty Research Group.

The results found that increases in Canadian regulatory bank capital requirement ratio led to a decrease in the volume of gross loan offered by Canadian banks to the non-financial sector, over the current year, considering macroeconomic control variables.

Keywords Basel Accords • Regulatory Capital Requirements • Canadian Bank Lending Behaviour • Canadian Bank Lending Volume • Macro-prudential Regulations • Microprudential Regulations • GDP • Bank Size • Bank Liquidity • Monetary Policy • Inflation Rate (CPI) • GDP Gap • Business Climate • and Credit-to-GDP Gap

B. Piper, *The Effect of Changes in Regulatory Capital Requirements on Banks Lending*
https://doi.org/10.1007/978-3-032-02208-0_2

2.1 Introduction

In this chapter, we analysed the effect of changes in Bank regulatory capital requirements on the lending volume of Canadian banks. To this aim, we used a sample of annual financial statistics of Canadian financial institutions from 2012 to 2021, from Fitch Connect database, encompassing Universal Commercial Banks, Wholesale Commercial Banks, Development Banks, as well as Trading and Investment Banks, representing 120 Canadian banks, and accounting for more than 90% of the Canadian banking sector, in terms of aggregate total assets over the period of 2012 to 2021.

Bank regulatory capital requirements have been used by financial regulators as a financial stability tool to ensure that banks remain resilient during times of economic downturn. Although increases in bank regulatory capital requirements by financial regulators have the benefit of stabilising the financial system, it does have adverse impacts on banks' lending. This study aims at investigating the impact of changes in Bank regulatory capital requirements on the lending volume of Canadian banks.

Previous empirical results from single-country studies suggest that increases in capital requirements reduced bank lending volume to firms and households. The literature review also indicates that there are very few single-country studies on the effect of regulatory capital requirements on bank lending volume. Additionally, there is no Canada-specific study on the effect of regulatory capital requirements on bank lending volume, at the time of this research. Aiyar et al. (2016) investigated the relationship between the UK's bank capital requirement regulation and bank lending volume. The results found that tightening capital requirements has a reducing impact on bank lending volume. The evidence suggests that banks in the UK react to tighter bank capital requirements by reducing the volume of loan offered to their clients.

Similarly, Noss and Toffano (2016) studied the impact of changes in banks' capital requirements on banks' lending in the UK. The results of their studies demonstrated that increasing aggregate bank capital requirements during an economic upswing led to a reduction in bank lending. They found that the reduction effect is higher for corporate bank lending, in comparison to bank lending to households. Meeks (2017) studied the macroeconomic effects of changes in microprudential bank capital requirements, using a dataset on the Basel I and Basel II regimes in the

UK. The study demonstrated that tighter regulatory capital requirements led to a decrease in bank lending to firms and households.

Behn et al. (2016) obtained similar results by investigating the procyclicality of capital regulation and lending in Germany. The result indicates that regulators tightened capital charges on loans by 0.5 percentage point to deal with the effects of exogenous shocks to the German economy after the Lehman Brothers collapse of September 2008. German banks reacted to the increase in regulatory capital charges on loans by 0.5 percentage point by reducing the amount of loans by 2.1–3.9 percentage points. These results indicate that microprudential capital regulations can have real effects on the volume of liquidity that banks decide to offer in credit facilities, following increases in regulatory capital requirements.

The lending behaviour of German banks following the tightening of regulatory capital requirements after the Lehman Brothers collapse in September 2008 does not appear to be an isolated scenario. The decrease in lending volumes in response to increases in capital requirements appears to be the natural response of banks to cope with higher levels of regulatory capital requirements. This type of bank lending behaviour suggests that microprudential regulations such as the tightening of regulatory capital requirements have the desire effect of stabilising the economy by reducing the level of liquidity available in the economy.

Bui et al. (2017) estimated the level of capital buffers required to reduce or attenuate the impact of system-wide losses, focusing on Australian banks. The study found that a moderate increase in capital buffers can have significant effects on the economy, such as maintaining the resilience of the financial system. Imbierowicz et al. (2018) analysed how banks' capital and lending decisions are impacted by changes in bank-specific capital and disclosure requirements. The results indicated a decrease in German banks' asset risk following increases in regulatory capital requirement ratio.

German banks also reduce the buffer between the actual and regulatory capital ratios. Uluc and Wieladek (2018) investigated the effects of changes to bank-specific capital requirements on mortgage loans, studying a dataset of all new mortgages issued in the UK between Q2 2005 and Q2 2007.

The results found that a rise of a 100 basis points in capital requirements led to a 4% decline in individual mortgage loan volume. Similar studies were conducted by Juelsrud and Wold (2020), and they found that in response to higher capital requirements, Norwegian banks raised loan interest rates and decreased corporate loan growth.

A capital buffer framework was introduced as part of Basel III. Capital buffers are additional buffers imposed on top of the minimum regulatory capital requirement to provide banks with sufficient resilience against economic and financial shocks. Jiménez et al. (2017) analysed the impact of macroprudential policy on credit supply cycles and real effects in Spain. They found that hiking the level of capital buffers on top of the minimum capital requirements resulted into an increase in lending volume. Specifically, they found that a 1 percentage point increase in capital buffers led to increases in credit to firms by 9 percentage points.

The literature contains various cross-country studies that analysed the effect of regulatory capital requirements and bank lending volume. Laidroo (2016) studied the factors that explain loan growth in foreign-owned banks, in comparison with privately owned domestic banks. The study found that regulatory capital requirements are an important factor of loan growth. Lee and Stebunovs (2016) analysed the effect of bank regulatory capital requirements on employment. They found that stricter capital requirements reduced employment in industries that lack substitutes for bank loans. These results suggest that tighter capital restrictions reduce the volume of credit offered by banks, leading to reduced investments and higher unemployment.

Cohen and Scatigna (2016) investigated bank ratios analysing a sample of 94 large banks in emerging economies. The results found that while banks continued with the expansion of their credit volume in response to higher levels of regulatory capital requirements, the growth rate of their lending volume was slower across European banks. Gopalakrishnan et al. (2021) investigated the impact of risk-sensitive Basel regulations on debt financing of corporations worldwide. They found that the implementation of Basel II regulations led to a decrease in credit for lower-rated firms. These results are in line with the results of existing studies on the relationship between bank capital and volume of credit.

Gambacorta and Murcia (2020) reviewed and analysed the results of a research project piloted by five Latin American central banks on the effectiveness of macroprudential policies and their interactions with monetary policy. The analysis found that macroprudential tools stabilised credit cycles. The effect of macroprudential tools on credit growth is stronger for tools targeting the curbing of the cycle, than for policies that focused on fostering economic resilience. Gropp et al. (2019) studied the impact of capital requirement regulations on banks' balance sheet, and their transmission to the real economy. They found that banks responded to tighter regulatory capital requirements by reducing their credit volume allocation to corporate and retail customers.

Kanngiesser et al. (2020) analysed the macroeconomic effects of shocks to bank capital buffers in the Euro zone. The results found that banks reduced lending and decreased their relative exposure to riskier assets in response to an increase in bank capital buffer. Broll et al. (2018), Brigida (2019), and Mankart et al. (2020) conducted a study of banks' risk-taking behaviour. The study found that tighter capital requirement regulations limit banks' ability to take on excessive risk. Furthermore, Deli and Hasan (2017) analysed the effect of a set of higher capital regulatory requirements on loan growth. The analysis found a negative relationship between bank capital requirement regulations and bank loan growth. Roulet (2018) found comparable results analysing the effect of Basel III regulations on bank lending activities.

In contrast to other studies, multiple cross-country studies found that regulatory capital requirements can have a positive impact on bank lending. Procyclicality is observed when key economic variables trend in the same direction as the overall economy. Ly and Shimizu (2021) analysed the procyclical effect of risk-sensitive capital requirement regulation on bank lending. They found that the risk-sensitive requirements of the Basel II and III capital requirements regulations have procyclical effects on bank lending in nine European countries. These findings suggest that tightening regulatory capital requirements under Basel II and Basel III capital regulations led to higher bank loan volume.

Regulators and policymakers should focus on setting capital buffers before economic downswings, rather than dampening excess cyclicality. Similar results were obtained by Bahaj and Malherbe (2020) who challenged the conventional wisdom that tighter capital requirements lead to increases in banks' lending rates, therefore lowering bank lending volume and dampening economic activity. Bahaj and Malherbe (2020) argued that higher cost of capital for banks and stricter regulatory capital requirements do not necessarily lead to a decrease in bank lending. Their results found that government guarantees represent a form of implicit subsidies offered to banks. While this subsidy is decreased through compliance with tighter regulatory capital requirements, the government guarantees also make banks underrate risky loans that generate surplus.

Bahaj and Malherbe (2020) agreed that increasing regulatory capital contributes to banks' safety. They characterised the interaction between government guarantees and regulatory capital requirements as the mechanism of the forced safety effect. Begenau (2020) designed a quantitative dynamic general equilibrium model based on the assumption that households' preferences for safe and liquid assets constitute a violation of the Modigliani and Miller model. The model indicated that the scarcity of coveted assets due to stricter regulatory bank capital requirements can lead to a decrease in overall bank funding costs and an increase of bank lending volume.

Our study focused on the Canadian commercial and development banking, trading, and investment banking sector, as it is the main driver of Canadian banks' loan to the non-financial sector, which ultimately supports the real economy. We adapted key aspects of pre-existing regression models applied in previous studies published by other scholars such as Aiyar et al. (2016), De Jonghe et al. (2020), and Imbierowicz et al. (2021).

Firstly, we found that a 1% increase in Canadian regulatory bank capital requirement ratio led to a 0.26% decrease in the volume of credit offered by Canadian banks to the non-financial sector, over the current year, considering macroeconomic control variables. These results were statistically significant. These findings are in line with previous results obtained by Aiyar et al. (2016), Gropp et al. (2019), De Jonghe et al. (2020), and Imbierowicz et al. (2021).

Secondly, we observed (Table 2.9) that a 1% increase in the lagged value of excess capital ratio led to a 0.07% increase in the volume of loan offered by Canadian banks to the non-financial sector, over the current year, considering macroeconomic control variables. While these findings may suggest that banks with excess capital can increase their volume of loan to the non-financial sector, even when subject to increases in capital requirements, the results were not statistically significant.

Thirdly, we observed (Table 2.9) that Canadian banks' lending volume to the non-financial sector decreased following increases in capital requirements, and the implementation of an unfavourable economic policy. Specifically, a 1% increase in capital requirements, followed by a 1% increase in the yearly average of Canada News-Based Policy Uncertainty Index (Economic Policy), led to a decrease in Canadian banks' lending volume by 0.05%. These results were statistically significant. These results indicated that the impact of changes in regulatory capital requirements on Canadian banks lending volume to the non-financial sector can be severe if the country is subject to the implementation of unfavourable economic policy. The objective of a favourable economic policy is the achievement of full employment, economic expansion, and growth, maintaining price stability through the application of monetary policy tools, and the implementation of an expansionary fiscal policy.

This suggests that the negative impact of tighter Canadian regulatory capital requirements on Canadian banks' lending volume to the non-financial sector can be attenuated by increasing regulatory capital requirements only when the economy is supported by a favourable economic policy, which objective is to achieve full employment, economic expansion and growth, maintaining price stability through the application of monetary policy tools, and the implementation of an expansionary fiscal policy.

Times of economic downturns, such as recessionary periods are characterised by high inflation, high interest rates, and high unemployment. These characteristics are contrary to the objective of a favourable economic policy. Therefore, we concluded that during times of economic distress, Canadian regulators should maintain Canadian regulatory capital requirements at levels equivalent or lower to those prior to the economic downturn period.

Regulatory capital requirements should only be increased prior or post-economic downturns when a combination of the following four favourable economic policy factors is fulfilled: (i) Full employment, (ii) Economic expansion and growth, (iii) Price stability through the application of monetary policy tools, and (iv) Expansionary fiscal policy. This will enable better mitigation of liquidity shocks during times of economic downturn, ensuring economic recovery efforts are not negatively impacted by the effects of stricter regulatory capital requirements.

Finally, our findings confirm the results of previous studies such as Aiyar et al. (2016), Gropp et al. (2019), De Jonghe et al. (2020), and Imbierowicz et al. (2021), and contribute to the scarce literature regarding the impact of regulatory capital requirements on the lending volume of banks.

Overall, our results provide regulators and policymakers with a combination of key economic factors necessary to ensure increases in regulatory capital requirements do not lead to tighter liquidity to the non-financial sector, which could negatively impact recovery efforts from an economic downturn. Our empirical results suggest that during times of economic downturn, Canadian regulators and policymakers should maintain Canadian regulatory capital requirements at levels equivalent or lower to those prior to the economic downturn. Regulators and policymakers should

- *Only tighten regulatory capital requirements* prior or post-economic downturns, when a *combination* of the following *four favourable economic policy factors* is fulfilled:
  - (i) Full employment,
  - (ii) Economic expansion and growth,
  - (iii) Price stability through the application of monetary policy tools, and
  - (iv) Expansionary fiscal policy.

The remainder parts of this study are structured as follows: Section 2.2 provides a brief description of capital requirement regulation in Canada, Section 2.3 provides details of research questions and hypotheses, Section 2.4 provides details on our sample data and variables, Section 2.5 presents empirical studies, Section 2.6 provides details of robustness checks, and Section 2.7 presents conclusions.

2.2 Capital Requirements Regulation in Canada

The OSFI is a member of the Basel Committee on Banking Supervision and contributed to the elaboration of the Basel framework. Subsections 485(1) and 949(1) of the Canadian Bank Act require banks and bank holding companies, as well as other FRFIs (trust companies and federally regulated loan companies) to maintain adequate capital reserves.[1] To this aim, OSFI regulates Canadian financial institutions and sets the level of capital requirements for Canadian banks by establishing minimum risk-based capital and leverage ratios.

The minimum risk-based capital and leverage ratios required by OSFI were established following the guidelines of the Basel Committee. Canadian capital adequacy and leverage requirements are applicable to Canadian financial institutions designated by OSFI as D-SIBs and SMSBs.[2] OSFI defines RWAs as the highest value of the sum of RWA for credit risk, RWA for market risk, and RWA for operational risk.[3] In addition to a minimum

[1] Office of the Superintendent of Financial Institutions, Overview of Risk-Based Capital Requirements. Available from https://www.osfi-bsif.gc.ca/Eng/fi-if/rg-ro/gdn-ort/gl-ld/Pages/CAR22_chpt1.aspx. July 2022.

[2] Office of the Superintendent of Financial Institutions. Overview of Risk-based Capital Requirements – Scope of Application. Available from https://www.osfi-bsif.gc.ca/Eng/fi-if/rg-ro/gdn-ort/gl-ld/Pages/CAR22_chpt1.aspx. July 2022.

[3] Office of the Superintendent of Financial Institutions. Overview of Risk-based Capital Requirements – Total Riskweighted Assets. Available from https://www.osfi-bsif.gc.ca/Eng/fi-if/rg-ro/gdn-ort/gl-ld/Pages/CAR22_chpt1.aspx. July 2022.

capital requirement sets at 8% of RWAs, OSFI also requires D-SIBs and SMSBs to maintain the following key mandatory capital buffers[4]:

- Levels of **Capital Adequacy Ratios** during periods of economic upswings that are higher than the minimum capital requirement. The OSFI minimum capital requirement is set at 8% of RWAs.
- In addition to the minimum capital requirements, a **Capital Conservation Buffer (CCB)** of 2.5% of RWAs, calculated using only Common Equity Tier 1 capital (CET1) is required. This translates into 10.5% of RWAs.
- A **Countercyclical Buffer** is set by OSFI to consider the Canadian macroeconomic and financial environment. Financial institutions can be subject to a countercyclical buffer up to 2.5% of RWAs.
- Designated financial institutions are required to maintain **D-SIB Surcharge**. The Bank of Montreal, Bank of Nova Scotia, Canadian Imperial Bank of Commerce, National Bank of Canada, Royal Bank of Canada, and Toronto-Dominion Bank have been designated by OSFI as D-SIBs and are required to maintain a CET1 surcharge of 1% of RWAs.
- A **DSB** of up to 2.5% of D-SIBs' RWAs is required. The DSB was established by OSFI to cover any vulnerabilities contained in the aforementioned capital requirements.

Figure 2.1 summarises and illustrates OSFI capital requirements in percentage of RWAs from DTIs.

2.3 Research Questions and Hypotheses

The literature review presented in the previous section revealed the existence of mixed results regarding the implications of changes in banks' regulatory capital requirements on banks' lending behaviour.

Furthermore, the literature review also revealed that there were no studies regarding the impact of regulatory capital requirements on the lending volume and rate of Canadian banks. The conclusions of the literature review led to the following research question:

[4] Office of the Superintendent of Financial Institutions. Overview of Risk-based Capital Requirements – Mandated Capital Buffers. Available from https://www.osfi-bsif.gc.ca/Eng/fi-if/rg-ro/gdn-ort/gl-ld/Pages/CAR22_chpt1.aspx. July 2022.

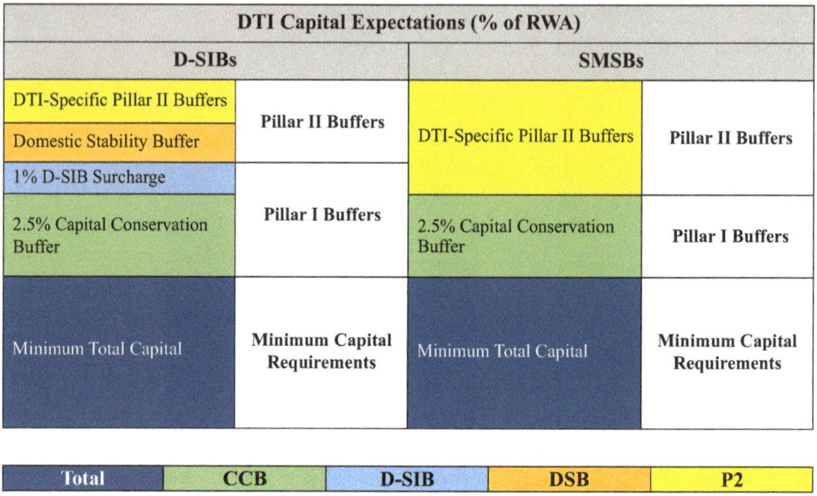

Fig. 2.1 OSFI capital requirements in percentage of RWAs from DTIs (Source: Office of the Superintendent of Financial Institutions, *Overview of Risk-Based Capital Requirements – Annex 2 Supervisory Target Capital Requirements*. Available from https://www.osfi-bsif.gc.ca/Eng/fi-if/rg-ro/gdn-ort/gl-ld/Pages/CAR22_chpt1.aspx, July 2022).

Figure 2: Summary of Research Question 1

Gap in Literature	**Research Question**	**Hypothesis**
▪ Mixed results regarding the implications of changes in banks' regulatory capital requirements on banks' lending behaviour. ▪ Limited literature regarding the impact of regulatory capital on lending volume and rates of Canadian banks.	What is the impact of banks' regulatory capital requirements on the Lending Volume of Canadian banks?	**H0**: Increase in banks' regulatory capital requirements **leads to a decrease** of Canadian banks lending volume. **H1**: Increase in banks' regulatory capital requirements **leads to an increase** of Canadian banks lending volume. **H2**: Increase in banks' regulatory capital requirements **leads to no impact** on Canadian banks lending volume.

Fig. 2.2 Summary of research question 1

- **Research Question 1:** *What is the impact of banks' regulatory capital requirements on the Lending Volume of Canadian banks?*

Figure 2.2 presents a summary of the first research question and relevant hypothesis.

2.4 Data and Variables

This study uses the annual financial statistics of Canadian financial institutions from 2012 to 2021, from Fitch Connect database.[5] The aggregate total asset value of the entire Canadian banking industry over the period of 2012 to 2021 is 5.2 trillion USD. Universal Commercial Banks, Wholesale Commercial Banks, Development Banks, Investment and Trading Banks hold 4.8 trillion USD in aggregate total assets, over the same period. Our sample covers Universal Commercial Banks, Wholesale Commercial Banks, Development Banks, and Investment and Trading Banks, representing 120 Canadian banks, and accounting for 92% of the Canadian banking sector, in terms of aggregate total assets over the period of 2012 to 2021. Our sample also covers GDP Gap statistics from the Bank of Canada,[6] Credit-to-GDP Gap statistics from the BIS,[7] Business Climate outlook statistics[8] from the Bank of Canada, and the Canada News-Based Policy Uncertainty Index from the Economic Policy Uncertainty Research Group,[9] from 2012 and 2021.

Our study focuses on the Canadian commercial, development, investment, and trading banking sector, given that it is the main vehicle of lending to the non-financial sector, which supports the real economy. Contrarily to the financial economy which covers transactions of money and financial assets, the real economy is more connected to economic growth, and encompasses the production and distribution of goods and services. Furthermore, corporate loans to the non-financial sector tend to have shorter debt maturities, aligning more with changes in regulatory capital requirements.

The study investigated the impact of changes in regulatory capital requirements on the lending volume of Canadian banks. We measured the change in lending volume of Canadian banks, calculating the annual variation in Canadian banks' gross loans to the non-financial sector.

[5] Fitch Solutions, Canadian Bank Financials Data, from 2012 to 2021. Available from Fitch Solutions. July 2022.

[6] Bank of Canada, Product Market: Definitions, Graphs and Data. Available from https://www.bankofcanada.ca/?p=39818. July 2022.

[7] The Bank for International Settlements, Credit-to-GDP Trend (HP Filter). Available from https://stats.bis.org/statx/srs/table/f2.1?p=20174&c=. July 2022.

[8] Bank of Canada, Business Outlook Survey Data. Available from https://www.bankofcanada.ca/publications/bos/business-outlook-survey-data/. July 2022.

[9] Economic Policy Uncertainty Research Group, News-Based Policy Uncertainty Index. Available from Economic Policy Uncertainty Index. July 2022.

The introduction of Basel III in 2010 required banks to maintain a minimum capital adequacy ratio of 8%, which is determined considering Tier 1 capital and Tier 2 capital only, eliminating Tier 3 capital from the capital adequacy ratio calculation.[10]

The OSFI[11] defines total regulatory capital as Tier 1 regulatory capital plus Tier 2 capital. Tier 1 regulatory capital is the aggregation of Common Equity Tier 1 (CET1) capital and Additional Tier 1 capital.

OSFI[12] defines Tier 2 capital (prior to regulatory adjustments) as the sum of the following items: Instruments issued by the financial institution that meet the criteria for inclusion in Tier 2 capital (and are not included in Tier 1 capital); Surplus (share premium) emanating from the issue of instruments included in Tier 2 capital; Instruments issued by consolidated subsidiaries of the financial institution and held by third parties that meet the criteria for inclusion in Tier 2 capital (and are not included in Tier 1 capital); and certain loan loss allowances that meet the criteria for inclusion in Tier 2 capital.

OSFI[13] defines total regulatory capital requirements (Total Reg Cap Ratio) as the sum of risk-based capital ratios, conservation buffer, and a countercyclical buffer (where applicable). Risk-based capital ratios are calculated by dividing total capital (Total Reg Cap) by the sum of credit, operational, and market RWAs. OSFI requires Canadian banks to maintain a minimum capital requirement ratio, in addition to a conservation buffer (where applicable), a countercyclical buffer (where applicable), and Basel III leverage ratio.

Canadian banks are regulated by the OSFI and are required to abide by regulatory capital requirements set by OSFI. Our study used the annual variation in (Total regulatory capital ratios + Basel III leverage

[10] Basel Committee on Banking Supervision, History of the Basel Committee (Basel III: Responding to the 2007-09 Financial Crisis). Available from https://www.bis.org/bcbs/history.htm. April 2022.

[11] Office of the Superintendent of Financial Institutions, Requirements for Inclusion in Regulatory Capital. Available from https://www.osfi-bsif.gc.ca/en/guidance/guidance-library/capital-adequacy-requirements-car-2024-chapter-2-definition-capital. July 2022.

[12] Office of the Superintendent of Financial Institutions, Tier 2 Capital. Available from https://www.osfi-bsif.gc.ca/en/guidance/guidance-library/capital-adequacy-requirements-car-2024-chapter-2-definition-capital. July 2022.

[13] Office of the Superintendent of Financial Institutions, Calculation of OSFI Minimum Capital Requirements. Available from https://www.osfi-bsif.gc.ca/Eng/fi-if/rg-ro/gdn-ort/gl-ld/Pages/CAR22_chpt1.aspx. July 2022.

ratios) disclosed to OSFI by Canadian banks, as part of their annual financial disclosure.

$$\Delta\,\text{in TotalReg Cap Ratio} = \Delta\,\text{in}\,\frac{\text{TotalReg Cap}}{\text{RWA}} + \Delta\,\text{in Basel III Ratio}$$

Our study used lagged values of Return on Assets, Ratio of Liquid Assets to Total Assets, Bank Size, Ratio of Core Deposits, and Excess Capital Ratio to account for bank effects.

Lagged (t–1) Return on Assets and Lagged (t–1) Ratio of Liquid Assets to Total Assets were calculated using the values of Return on Assets and Ratio of Liquid Assets to Total Assets, disclosed by the Canadian bank in the previous year (t–1).

Lagged (t–1) Ratio of Core Deposits was obtained by using the lagged Ratio of Total Customer Deposits to Total Assets.

Lagged (t–1) Bank Size is the lagged value of the logarithm of Total Assets.

Basel III[14] requires banks to maintain additional countercyclical capital buffers for times of economic downturn. The percentage of countercyclical capital buffers could range between 0 and 2.5%. Under Basel III, the local banking supervision regulator (OSFI for Canadian banks) could opt for the imposition of the highest required countercyclical capital buffer of 2.5%, leading to a minimum capital adequacy ratio of 10.5%. We calculated the lagged excess capital ratio (Lagged Ex Cap Ratio) by subtracting the minimum capital adequacy ratio of 10.5% under Basel III (Min Basel III Cap Ratio of 10.5%) from the total regulatory capital ratio of the bank and lagging the result.

$$\text{Lagged}\,(t-1)\ \text{Ex Cap Ratio} = \text{Lagged}\,(t-1)\ [\text{Total Reg Cap Ratio} - \text{Min Basel III Cap Ratio of }10.5\%]$$

Variables measuring Economic Policy, GDP Gap, Business Climate, and Credit-to-GDP Gap were introduced to control for macroeconomic effects.

Economic Policy is measured using the yearly average of Canada News-Based Policy Uncertainty Index, published by the Economic Policy Uncertainty Research Group.[15]

[14] Basel Committee on Banking Supervision, The Capital Buffers in Basel III – Executive Summary. Available from https://www.bis.org/bcbs/history.htm. July 2022.

[15] Economic Policy Uncertainty Research Group, News-Based Policy Uncertainty Index. Available from Economic Policy Uncertainty Index. July 2022.

GDP Gap is measured by yearly average of output gap, which is the deviation of actual GDP from potential output, published by the Bank of Canada.[16]

Credit-to-GDP Gap is measured by the delta between credit-to-GDP ratio and its long-term trend, published by the BIS.[17]

Business Climate is measured by the yearly Business Outlook Survey indicator, published by the Bank of Canada.[18]

A fixed effect model (Panel Data Regression) enables the control for all time-invariant differences between observed entities. This ensures that the coefficients of the time effect model are not biased due to the non-inclusion or omission of time-invariant characteristics of the entity.

In the case of our research, the time-invariant characteristics could be the bank's corporate culture, bank's internal policy, and bank's management strategy.

However, time-invariant characteristics such as bank's corporate culture, bank's internal policy, and bank's management strategy could also be classified as time-variant characteristics. Bank's corporate culture, bank's internal policy, and bank's management strategy could be modified multiple times during a year.

In the empirical study, we included bank control variables which are the results of the bank's corporate culture, bank's internal policy, and bank's management strategy.

In the empirical study of the impact of changes in bank regulatory capital requirements on the lending volume of Canadian banks, the bank control variables account for lagged values of Excess capital, Return on Assets, Ratio of Liquid Assets to Total Assets, Bank Size, and Ratio of Core Deposits.

The values of the bank control variables incorporate the effect of banks' internal characteristics. Furthermore, given that the differences between the banks (entities) are correlated with predictors (bank control variables), a random effect model (Panel Model Regression) does not emerge as an option.

[16] Bank of Canada, Product Market: Definitions, Graphs and Data. Estimates of the Output Gap. Available from https://www.bankofcanada.ca/?p=39818. July 2022.

[17] The Bank for International Settlements, Credit-to-GDP Trend (HP Filter). Available from https://stats.bis.org/statx/srs/table/f2.1?p=20174&c=. July 2022.

[18] Bank of Canada, Business Outlook Survey Data. Available from https://www.bankofcanada.ca/publications/bos/business-outlook-survey-data/. July 2022.

Komath et al. (2023) studied the impact of corporate governance and related controversies on the market value of banks. They found a statistically significant relationship between the corporate governance controversies scores and the market value of banks.

Barth and Mansouri (2021) studied the role of corporate culture in banking. They found that corporate culture is a softer aspect of governance necessary to enhance banking stability. Specifically, they found that banks with a more pronounced competition-oriented culture have stronger bonus-focused compensation schemes. Banks with a strong focus on growth demonstrated higher stock returns, and finally, banks with a focus on stability had lower bankruptcy risk.

Table 2.1 presents a summarised description of variables.

The statistics on the volume of credit offered by Canadian banks to the non-financial sector showed some spurious outliers. Hence, we transformed the statistics through winsorisation to limit the effect of extreme values or spurious outliers.

Table 2.2 presents descriptive statistics following winsorisation.

Table 2.2 (Descriptive Statistics) shows that the volume of credit offered by Canadian banks to the non-financial sector increased by 5.78% on average in a year, while the yearly change in regulatory capital requirements is 2.28% on average, and the level of excess capital for the previous year increased by 27.27% on average.

Table 2.3 presents the annual average change in regulatory capital requirements and the annual average change in Canadian banks' gross loan to the non-financial sector, following winsorisation.

The annual average change in regulatory capital requirements and the annual average change in Canadian banks' gross loan to the non-financial sector, following winsorisation (Table 2.3), indicate that increases in regulatory capital requirements only led to a decrease in banks' loan volume during the years 2014 and 2015. However, further analysis is necessary to ascertain the true impact of regulatory capital requirements on Canadian banks' lending volume. The subsequent pages will provide a detailed empirical study.

2.5 Results

We analysed the effect of changes in regulatory capital requirements on the volume of credit offered by Canadian banks to the non-financial sector. Our empirical studies adapted pre-existing models, previously applied

Table 2.1 Description of variables

	Definition	*Data Source*
Dependent Variable		
Annual Δ Bank Lending Volume	Annual Δ in Canadian Banks' Gross Loans to the non-financial sector.	Fitch Connect Database
Independent Variable		
Annual Δ Canadian Bank Capital Requirements	Annual variation in (Total regulatory capital ratios + Basel III leverage ratios) disclosed to OSFI by Canadian banks, as part of their annual financial disclosure.	Fitch Connect Database
Bank Control Variables		
Lagged (t–1) Excess capital	Lagged excess capital ratio is calculated by subtracting the minimum capital adequacy ratio of 10.5% under Basel III from the Total regulatory capital ratio of the bank (Total Reg Cap Ratio) and taking the lagged value of the result. We adopted a conservative approach for the calculation of Lagged (t–1) Excess capital by utilising the most stringent minimum capital requirement.	Fitch Connect Database
Lagged (t–1) Return on Assets	Lagged Return on Assets	Fitch Connect Database
Lagged (t–1) Ratio of Liquid Assets to Total Assets	Lagged Ratio of Liquid Assets to Total Assets	Fitch Connect Database
Lagged (t–1) Bank Size	Lagged Logarithm of Total Assets	Fitch Connect Database
Lagged (t–1) Ratio of Core Deposit	Lagged Ratio of Total Core Deposits (Total Customer Deposits) to Total Assets	Fitch Connect Database
Macroeconomic Control Variables		
Economic Policy	Yearly Average of Canada News-Based Policy Uncertainty Index	Economic Policy Uncertainty Research Group
GDP Gap	Deviation of actual GDP from potential output (Yearly Average of output gap)	Bank of Canada
Business Climate	Canadian Business Outlook Survey (BOS) Indicator (Yearly Average of BOS Indicator)	Bank of Canada
Credit-to-GDP Gap	Deviation of credit to GDP from its long-term trend (BIS Statistics)	Bank for International Settlements (BIS)

Table 2.2 Descriptive statistics

	Mean	*Standard Deviation*
Dependent Variable		
Annual Δ Bank Lending Volume	5.78	18.27
Independent Variable		
Annual Δ Canadian Bank Capital Requirements	2.28	12.90
Bank Control Variables		
Lagged (t–1) Excess capital	27.27	23.95
Lagged (t–1) Return on Assets	0.57	0.84
Lagged (t–1) Ratio of Liquid Assets to Total Assets	23.31	26.76
Lagged (t–1) Bank Size	3.53	1.04
Lagged (t–1) Ratio of Core Deposits	64.13	26.78
Macroeconomic Control Variables		
Economic Policy	262.88	88.24
GDP Gap	–1.84	2.02
Business Climate	0.02	1.78
Credit-to-GDP Gap	203.7	16.59
Other Details		
Observations		256

Note: Shown are descriptive statistics using financial statistics of Canadian financial institutions and macroeconomic data, from 2012 to 2021, for variables described in Table 2.1.

Table 2.3 Annual average of changes in regulatory capital requirements and Canadian banks' gross loan

Year	*Mean of Annual Δ Canadian Bank Capital Requirements*	*Mean of Annual Δ Bank Lending Volume*
2012	–	–
2013	12.51	3.54
2014	**11.40**	**–1.01**
2015	**2.89**	**–3.84**
2016	3.2	9.26
2017	1.70	13.20
2018	–0.69	4.26
2019	3.62	6.86
2020	2.22	5.96
2021	2.72	17.18

Note: Shown are the average change in regulatory capital requirements and the average change in Canadian banks' gross loan to the non-financial sector, annually, following winsorisation.

by other researchers such as Aiyar et al. (2016), De Jonghe et al. (2020), and Imbierowicz et al. (2021), for the study of changes of capital requirements and bank lending in other jurisdictions, other than Canada.

The adaptation of pre-existing models ensures our studies follow a scientific rigour and enables the comparison of our results with those from previous studies. Our model is also the result of the application of econometric methods and principles from Gourieroux and Jasiak (2018), Campbell et al. (1996), as well as research methods' recommendations from Chevalier et al. (2019).

Additionally, our model is also the result of the application of knowledge acquired through the literature review, as well as professional and managerial experiences. The validity and goodness-of-fit of our model is demonstrated through the model statistics, regression assumption tests and robustness tests presented in subsequent sections.

Adapting pre-existing models used by Aiyar et al. (2016), De Jonghe et al. (2020), and Imbierowicz et al. (2021), we studied the transmission of changes of Canadian regulatory capital requirements to Canadian banks' lending volume, applying the following multiple regression model:

$$\Delta \mathbf{Y}_{\mathbf{a,t}} = \propto_0 + \sum_{t=1}^{t=10} \alpha_{1.t} \Delta \mathbf{Cap}_{\mathbf{a,t}} + \beta \mathbf{X}_{\mathbf{a,t-1}} + f_a + \varepsilon_{a,t} \qquad \text{(Model 1)}$$

where

$\Delta \mathbf{Y}_{\mathbf{a,t}}$ is the variation (year over year change) in Canadian bank 'a' lending volume following changes in regulatory capital requirements in year 't'. It is the measure of the change in lending volume of Canadian banks, calculated as the annual variation in Canadian banks' gross loans to the non-financial sector.

$\Delta \mathbf{Cap}_{\mathbf{a,t}}$ is the change in Regulatory bank capital requirement ratio for bank 'a', during year 't'. $\Delta \mathbf{Cap}_{\mathbf{a,t}}$ is calculated using the annual variation in (Total regulatory capital ratios + Basel III leverage ratios) disclosed to OSFI by Canadian banks, as part of their annual financial disclosure.

$$\Delta \text{in Total Reg Cap Ratio} = \Delta \text{in} \frac{\text{Total Reg Cap}}{\text{RWA}} + \Delta \text{in Basel III Leverage Ratio}$$

We introduced a vector of lagged bank-specific variables to control for bank effects. $\mathbf{X}_{\mathbf{a,t-1}}$ represents a vector of lagged bank-specific control variables, capturing the level of Excess Capital, Return on Assets, Ratio of Liquid Assets to Total Assets, Bank Size, and Ratio of core Deposits to Total Assets.

The lagged value of Excess Capital Ratio (Lagged (t–1) Ex Cap Ratio) was calculated by subtracting the minimum capital adequacy ratio of 10.5% under Basel III (Min Basel III Cap Ratio of 10.5%) from the Total regulatory capital ratio of the bank and lagging the value of the result (Lagged (t–1) Total Reg Cap Ratio).

The lagged values of Return on Assets and Ratio of Liquid Assets to Total Assets were calculated using the values of Return on Assets and Ratio of Liquid Assets to Total Assets, disclosed by the Canadian bank in the previous year (t–1).

The lagged value of Bank Size is the lagged value of the logarithm of Total Assets.

The lagged value of Ratio of Core Deposit was obtained by using the lagged ratio of Total Customer Deposits to Total Assets.

f_a is the vector of macroeconomic control variables introduced to control for macroeconomic effects. Variables measuring Economic Policy, GDP Gap, Business Climate, and Credit-to-GDP Gap were introduced to control for macroeconomic effects.

Table 2.4 presents the results of the multiple regression analysing the effect of the changes in regulatory capital requirements on the volume of credit offered by Canadian banks to the non-financial sector.

We tested regression assumptions supporting our multiple regression model. Table 2.5 presents the results of the Shapiro–Wilk W test for normal data.

The *p* value of the Shapiro–Wilk W test (*p* value of 0.00) confirmed that r is not normally distributed. Therefore, we conducted a non-parametric test (Kruskal–Wallis) to control for non-normality. Table 2.6 presents the results of the Kruskal–Wallis equality-of-populations rank test.

The *p* value (>0.05) of the Kruskal–Wallis equality-of-populations rank test is 0.70. Therefore, the null hypothesis is accepted, and we can confirm that the yearly change in Canadian Bank lending volume and yearly change in total bank capital requirement ratios follow the same statistical distribution.

Table 2.7 presents the results of the test of autocorrelation (Breusch–Godfrey LM Test).

The *p* value (>0.05) of the Breusch–Godfrey LM is 0.49. Therefore, the null hypothesis is accepted, and we can confirm that there is no serial correlation (no autocorrelation).

Table 2.4 Impact of changes in bank regulatory capital requirements on the lending volume of Canadian banks (multiple regression)

	Annual Δ Bank Lending Volume
Independent Variable	
Annual Δ Canadian Bank Capital Requirements Ratio	**−0.26 (0.003)***
Bank Control Variables	
Lagged (t−1) Excess capital	0.07 (0.42)
Lagged (t−1) Return on Assets	**−4.59 (0.005)***
Lagged (t−1) Ratio of Liquid Assets to Total Assets	−0.08 (0.17)
Lagged (t−1) Bank Size	**−2.21 (0.10)***
Lagged (t−1) Ratio of Core Deposits	−0.04 (0.39)
Macroeconomic Control Variables	
Economic Policy	**−0.05 (0.03)****
GDP Gap	−0.60 (0.44)
Business Climate	0.64 (0.57)
Credit-to-GDP Gap	0.28 (0.27)
Other Details	
Observations	256
Number of banks	120
R^2	0.1796
Prob > F	0.0000

Note: Shown are results of the multiple regression analysis using the multiple regression model presented above. The statistical significance of results is indicated by *10% level, **5% level and ***1% level using standard errors. *p* values are presented in parentheses after coefficient estimates.

Table 2.5 Shapiro–Wilk W test for normal data

Variable	*Obs*	*W*	*V*	*Z*	*Prob>z*
R	256	0.94	10.37	5.45	0.00000

Table 2.8 presents the results of the test of multicollinearity.

We tested for multicollinearity using the VIF, which measures the value of multicollinearity amongst regression variables. The test found a VIF value of 2.76 (<10), indicating that there is no multicollinearity.

Table 2.9 presents the results of the test of homoscedasticity of residuals (Breusch–Pagan/Cook–Weisberg test).

The *p* value of the Cameron & Trivedi's decomposition of IM test, and White's test for heteroscedasticity is 0.00. Therefore, the null hypothesis is rejected, and we can confirm that the variance of residuals is not homogenous (heteroscedasticity). The presence of heteroscedasticity could be due subpopulation differences, model misspecifications, or measurement errors. Therefore, we re-estimated the initial model, introducing robust standard errors to correct the effects of heteroscedasticity.

Table 2.6 Non-parametric test to control for non-normality (Kruskal–Wallis equality-of-populations rank test)

Chi2	*Prob*
Chi2 (226) = 214.10	0.70
Chi2 (226) with ties = 214.16	0.70

Note: Kruskal–Wallis equality-of-populations rank test for yearly Change in Canadian Bank lending volume and yearly Change in total bank capital requirement ratios.

Table 2.7 Test of autocorrelation (Breusch–Godfrey LM test)

lags(p)	*chi2*	*df*	*Prob > chi2*
1	0.46	1	0.49

Table 2.8 Test of multicollinearity (variance inflation factor (VIF))

Results - Test of Multicollinearity
Mean VIF = 2.76

Table 2.9 Test of homoscedasticity of residuals (Cameron & Trivedi's decomposition of IM test & White's test)

	chi2	*df*	*p*
Cameron & Trivedi's Decomposition of IM Test			
Heteroscedasticity	200.12	70	0.0000
White's Test			
H0: Homoscedasticity	chi2(59) = 141.54		
Ha: Unrestricted heteroscedasticity	Prob > chi2 = 0.00		

Table 2.10 presents the results of the multiple regression analysing the effect of changes in regulatory capital requirements on the volume of credit offered by Canadian banks to the non-financial sector, with the introduction of robust standard errors.

The *p* values related to the robust standard errors (Table 2.10) are different to the *p* values related to the standard errors obtained in the initial model estimation (Table 2.4). The issue of heteroscedasticity has been resolved, with the introduction of robust standard errors.

Table 2.10 Impact of changes in bank regulatory capital requirements on the lending volume of Canadian banks, with the introduction of robust standard errors

	Annual Δ Bank Lending Volume
Independent Variable	
Annual Δ Canadian Bank Capital Requirements Ratio	**−0.26** **(0.06)***
Bank Control Variables	
Lagged (t−1) Excess capital	0.07 (0.53)
Lagged (t−1) Return on Assets	**−4.59** **(0.03)****
Lagged (t−1) Ratio of Liquid Assets to Total Assets	−0.08 (0.26)
Lagged (t−1) Bank Size	**−2.21** **(0.09)***
Lagged (t−1) Ratio of Core Deposits	−0.04 (0.50)
Macroeconomic Control Variables	
Economic Policy	**−0.05** **(0.06)***
GDP Gap	−0.60 (0.36)
Business Climate	0.64 (0.59)
Credit-to-GDP Gap	0.28 (0.31)
Other Details	
Observations	256
Number of banks	120
R^2	0.1796
Prob > F	0.0000

Note: Shown are the results of the multiple regression analysis using the multiple regression model presented above and introducing robust standard errors. The statistical significance of results is indicated by *10% level, **5% level and ***1% level using robust standard errors. *p* values are presented in parentheses after coefficient estimates.

The results (Table 2.10) found that increases in Canadian regulatory capital requirements ratio have a negative effect on the volume of credit offered by Canadian banks to the non-financial sector during the same year. These results are consistent with findings from previous studies published by Aiyar et al. (2016), Gropp et al. (2019), De Jonghe et al. (2020), and Imbierowicz et al. (2021). The multiple regression coefficient indicates that a 1% increase in Canadian regulatory bank capital requirement ratio led to a 0.26% decrease in the volume of credit offered by Canadian banks to the non-financial sector, over the current year, considering macroeconomic control variables. These results were statistically significant.

Previous studies found that the effects of changes in bank capital requirements are subject bank characteristics. De Jonghe et al. (2020) found that increasing capital requirements translates into a decrease in lending volume of credit offered by riskier banks. Imbierowicz et al. (2021) confirmed that for weaker banks, increasing capital requirements leads to a decrease in their corporate loan volume. Under Basel III, banks are required to maintain additional countercyclical capital buffers, ranging between 0 and 2.5%, for times of economic downturn.

Following the Basel III requirement, the OSFI could require that banks maintain the highest countercyclical capital buffer of 2.5%, leading to a minimum capital adequacy ratio of 10.5%. We obtained the lagged excess capital ratio by subtracting the minimum capital adequacy ratio of 10.5% under Basel III from the total regulatory capital ratio of the bank and lagging the results. This ensures we capture the lagged value of excess capital ratio, based on regulatory recommendations.

The regression indicates that a 1% increase in the lagged (t–1) value of excess capital ratio led to a 0.07% increase in the volume of credit offered by Canadian banks to the non-financial sector, over the current year, considering macroeconomic control variables. While these results indicate that banks with excess capital may be able to increase their volume of credit to the non-financial sector, when subject to increases in capital requirements, the results were not statistically significant.

Furthermore, the regression found that Canadian banks' lending volume to the non-financial sector decreased following increases in capital requirements, and the implementation of an unfavourable economic policy. Specifically, a 1% increase in capital requirements, followed by a 1% increase in the yearly average of Canada News-Based Policy Uncertainty Index (Economic Policy) led to a decrease in Canadian banks' lending volume by 0.05% (Table 2.10). These results suggest that the effect of changes in regulatory capital requirements on Canadian banks' gross lending volume to the non-financial sector could be reduced if the country is subject to the implementation of a favourable economic policy. A favourable economic policy aims at achieving full employment, economic expansion, and growth, maintaining price stability through the application of monetary policy tools, and the implementation of an expansionary fiscal policy.

Therefore, our results suggest that increases in Canadian banks' gross lending volume to the non-financial sector, following increases in Canadian regulatory capital requirement ratios are conditioned by the fulfilment of a combination of the following four favourable economic policy factors: (i) Full employment, (ii) Economic expansion and growth, (iii) Price stability through the application of monetary policy tools, and (iv) Expansionary fiscal policy.

Times of economic downturns, such as recessionary periods, are marked by high inflation, high interest rates, and high unemployment. These characteristics are contrary to the objective of a favourable economic policy. Hence, it can be deducted that during times of economic downturn, Canadian regulators should maintain Canadian regulatory capital requirements at levels equivalent or lower to those of prior to the economic downturn period. Regulatory capital requirements should only be increased prior or post-economic downturns, when all four conditions listed above are met. This will ensure liquidity shocks during the time of economic downturn are mitigated and economic recovery is not halted.

2.6 Robustness Tests

We performed a series of robustness checks to assess for the sensitivity of our results to changes in variables, model composition, and sample. Hence, we re-performed the multiple regression model (Model 1, Table 2.10) using different subsamples. Firstly, we re-estimated the multiple regression model, excluding bank control variables.

Table 2.11 presents the results of robustness check, evaluating the impact of changes in bank regulatory capital requirements on the lending volume of Canadian banks, excluding bank control variables.

The results (Table 2.11) of the robustness check evaluating the impact of changes in bank regulatory capital requirements on the lending volume of Canadian banks, excluding bank control variables, align with those previously obtained through the initial estimation of the multiple regression model (Model 1, Table 2.10).

Secondly, we re-estimated the multiple regression model, excluding macroeconomic control variables. Table 2.12 presents the results of the robustness check, evaluating the impact of changes in bank regulatory capital requirements on the lending volume of Canadian banks, excluding macroeconomic control variables.

The results (Table 2.13) of the robustness check evaluating the impact of changes in bank regulatory capital requirements on the lending volume of Canadian banks, excluding macroeconomic control variables, align with those previously obtained through the initial estimation of the multiple regression model (Model 1, Table 2.10).

Table 2.11 Impact of changes in bank regulatory capital requirements on the lending volume of Canadian banks, excluding bank control variables

	Annual Δ Bank Lending Volume
Independent Variable	
Annual Δ Canadian Bank Capital Requirements	**−0.30** **(0.001)*****
Bank Control Variables	
Lagged (t−1) Excess capital	Excluded
Lagged (t−1) Return on Assets	Excluded
Lagged (t−1) Ratio of Liquid Assets to Total Assets	Excluded
Lagged (t−1) Bank Size	Excluded
Lagged (t−1) Ratio of Core Deposits	Excluded
Macroeconomic Control Variables	
Economic Policy	**−0.06** **(0.02)****
GDP Gap	−0.62 (0.44)
Business Climate	0.49 (0.67)
Credit-to-GDP Gap	0.29 (0.27)
Other Details	
Observations	258
Number of banks	120
R^2	0.0964
Prob > F	0.0001

Note: The statistical significance of results is indicated by *10% level, **5% level and ***1% level using standard errors. *p* values are presented in parentheses after coefficient estimates.

Thirdly, we re-estimated the multiple regression model, excluding bank control variables, and macroeconomic control variables. Table 2.13 presents the results of the robustness check evaluating the impact of changes in bank regulatory capital requirements on the lending volume of Canadian banks, excluding bank control variables, and macroeconomic control variables.

The results (Table 2.13) of the robustness check evaluating the impact of changes in bank regulatory capital requirements on the lending volume of Canadian banks, excluding bank control, and macroeconomic control variables, align with those previously obtained through the initial estimation of the multiple regression model (Model 1, Table 2.10).

Table 2.12 Impact of changes in bank regulatory capital requirements on the lending volume of Canadian banks, excluding macroeconomic control variables

	Annual Δ Bank Lending Volume	
Independent Variable		
Annual Δ Canadian Bank Capital Requirements	**−0.26** **(0.004)***	
Bank Control Variables		
Lagged (t–1) Excess capital	0.08 (0.40)	
Lagged (t–1) Return on Assets	**−5.15** **(0.002)***	
Lagged (t–1) Ratio of Liquid Assets to Total Assets	−0.09 (0.14)	
Lagged (t–1) Bank Size	−1.84 (0.18)	
Lagged (t–1) Ratio of Core Deposits	−0.05 (0.37)	
Macroeconomic Control Variables		
Economic Policy	Excluded	
GDP Gap	Excluded	
Business Climate	Excluded	
Credit-to-GDP Gap	Excluded	
Other Details		
Observations		256
Number of banks		120
R^2		0.1264
Prob > F		0.0000

Note: The statistical significance of results is indicated by *10% level, **5% level and ***1% level using standard errors. *p* values are presented in parentheses after coefficient estimates.

Table 2.13 Impact of changes in bank regulatory capital requirements on the lending volume of Canadian banks, excluding bank control and macroeconomic control variables

	Annual Δ Bank Lending Volume
Independent Variable	
Annual Δ Canadian Bank Capital Requirements	**–0.29** (0.001)***
Bank Control Variables	
Lagged (t–1) Excess capital	Excluded
Lagged (t–1) Return on Assets	Excluded
Lagged (t–1) Ratio of Liquid Assets to Total Assets	Excluded
Lagged (t–1) Bank Size	Excluded
Lagged (t–1) Ratio of Core Deposits	Excluded
Macroeconomic Control Variables	
Economic Policy	Excluded
GDP Gap	Excluded
Business Climate	Excluded
Credit-to-GDP Gap	Excluded
Other Details	
Observations	258
Number of banks	120
R^2	0.0396
Prob > F	0.0013

Note: The statistical significance of results is indicated by *10% level, **5% level and ***1% level using standard errors. *p* values are presented in parentheses after coefficient estimates.

2.7 Conclusion and Managerial Recommendation

This study investigated the effect of changes in regulatory capital requirements on the volume of credit offered by Canadian banks to the non-financial sector. The results suggest that increases in Canadian regulatory bank capital requirement ratio led to a decrease in the volume of credit offered by Canadian banks to the non-financial sector, over the current year, considering macroeconomic control variables. These results confirm that hypotheses H1 and H2 were rejected, in favour of hypothesis H0.

Overall, our results offer regulators and policymakers with a combination of key economic determinants, necessary to ensure increases in regulatory capital requirements do not lead to tighter liquidity to the non-financial sector, which could negatively impact recovery efforts targeting an economic downturn. The results suggest that the negative impact of tighter Canadian regulatory capital requirements on Canadian banks' lending volume to the non-financial sector can be soften by the fulfilment of a combination of the following four favourable economic policy factors: (i) Full employment, (ii) Economic expansion and growth, (iii) Price stability through the application of monetary policy tools, and (iv) Expansionary fiscal policy. The Appendix provides a detailed summary of the managerial recommendations.

Therefore, it can be deducted that during times of economic downturn, Canadian regulators and policymakers should maintain Canadian regulatory capital requirements at levels equivalent or lower to those of prior to the economic downturn period.

Furthermore, regulators and policymakers should only tighten regulatory capital requirements prior or post-economic downturns, when all four conditions listed above are met. This will ensure liquidity shocks during times of economic downturn are mitigated and economic recovery is not halted.

Our studies were limited by the existence of missed values, and a sample that only covered the period post-subprime crisis (2012 to 2021). Theoretically, we have 1200 observations (120 Canadian banks observed over 10 years). However, STATA only counts the number of observations for which there are values for all variables and years. Other limitations related to the presence of spurious outliers were mitigated by winsorising the samples utilised for the study of the research question.

Finally, future studies should investigate how factors such as bank lending interest rate, and bank lending portfolio are impacted by increases in regulatory capital requirements.

Therefore, Chapter 3 will study the impact of bank regulatory capital requirements on Canadian banks' gross loan interest rates.

CHAPTER 3

Impact of Bank Regulatory Capital Requirements: On Canadian Banks' Gross Loan Interest Rates

Abstract This chapter studied the impact of changes in regulatory capital requirements on the interest rates charged on gross loans offered by Canadian banks to the non-financial sector, using econometric methodologies.

The study used a sample of annual financial statistics of Canadian financial institutions from 2012 to 2021, from Fitch Connect database, over the period of 2012 to 2021. The data also encompasses macroeconomic statistics from the Bank of Canada, BIS, and Economic Policy Uncertainty Research Group.

The results found that increases in regulatory capital requirements did not impact loan interest rates during normal economic times, characterised with economic growth and expansion. The findings aligned with the results of Brei and Moreno (2019) who found that increases in regulatory capital requirements only led to increases in loan interest rates during times of large capital inflows, and not during normal economic times.

Keywords Basel Accords • Regulatory Capital Requirements • Canadian Bank Lending Behaviour • Canadian Bank Lending Interest • Macroprudential Regulations • Microprudential Regulations • GDP •

B. Piper, *The Effect of Changes in Regulatory Capital Requirements on Banks Lending*
https://doi.org/10.1007/978-3-032-02208-0_3

Bank Size • Bank Liquidity • Monetary Policy • Inflation Rate (CPI) • GDP Gap, Business Climate • and Credit-to-GDP Gap

3.1 Introduction

In this chapter, we analysed the impact of changes in regulatory capital requirements on the interest rates charged on loans offered by Canadian banks to the non-financial sector. To this aim, we used a sample of annual financial statistics of Canadian financial institutions from 2012 to 2021, from Fitch Connect database, covering Universal Commercial Banks, Wholesale Commercial Banks, Development Banks, as well as Trading and Investment Banks, representing 120 Canadian banks, and accounting for more than 90% of the Canadian banking sector, in terms of aggregate total assets over the period of 2012 to 2021.

Bank regulatory capital requirements have been used by financial regulators as a financial stability tool to ensure banks remain resilient during times of economic downturn. This study aims to investigate the impact of changes in Bank regulatory capital requirements on the lending interest rates charged by Canadian banks.

Bank loan rates, also known as bank interest rates, represent the value charged by banks on loan offers to corporations and households. Borrowers maintain their debt by paying fees in form of banks interest rate. Banks' rate spreads resulted from the difference between the interest rate that banks charge borrowers and the interest rate that banks offer to depositors. This is also known as the delta between the ask and bid prices. Hence, increases in spreads mean increases in credit risks and increases in interest rates.

Previous empirical results from single-country studies by Bichsel et al. (2021) on the effect of higher bank capital requirements on lending spreads in Switzerland found a positive correlation between capital ratios (actual and required) and lending spreads. Mainly, the results showed that a 1 percentage point increase of capital ratios (risk-weighted) led to an increase in lending spreads between 0 and 5 basis points. The effect is higher (between 5 and 20 basis points) for unweighted capital ratios (leverage ratios). The results indicate that increasing bank capital requirements leads to higher bank loan interest rates, considering that capital ratios (risk-weighted) also known as the capital adequacy ratio (CAR) or capital to RWA ratio (CRAR), measures bank minimum capital requirements.

Similarly, Glancy and Kurtzman (2018) examined how banks' loan rates reacted to a 50% increase in capital requirements for a subcategory of construction lending, High Volatility Commercial Real Estate (HVCRE) in the USA. The results found that a 1 percentage point increase in minimum capital requirement led to increases on loan rates by 9.5 basis points.

Furthermore, Juelsrud and Wold (2020), using data from the 2013 Norwegian policy reform, examined banks' reaction to an increase in capital requirements and how these adjustments transmit to the real economy. The analysis found that banks reacted to higher capital requirements by increasing interest rates. Additionally, Bolton et al. (2016) examined how relationship lending and transaction lending vary over the business cycle in Italy. They found that relationship banks demanded a higher interest spread before the crisis, offered more favourable continuation-lending terms, following the crisis, and registered fewer defaults.

The literature contains various cross-country studies that analysed the effect of regulatory capital requirements and bank lending interest rates. Benetton et al. (2021) analysed the transmission of changes in capital requirements to mortgage rates. The results showed that a 1 percentage point decrease in risk-weighted capital requirement led to a decrease in loan rates by approximately 10–16 basis points. The impact is higher for less-capitalised lenders. These results confirm the importance of using countercyclical regulatory capital requirements to support lending activities in time of economic downturn.

Similar results were obtained by Brei and Moreno (2019) who studied how banks modified their loan rates and deposit rates, following variations in regulatory capital requirements. The results found that higher capital requirements led to decreased deposit rates, while bank loan rates were kept static during normal economic times. These results indicate that higher bank capital requirements only led to higher loan rates in times of economic downturn.

Gambacorta and Shin (2018) studied why bank regulatory capital requirements is important for the effectiveness of monetary policy. Their results showed that a 1 percentage point increase in the equity-to-total assets ratio led to a 4 basis point decrease in the cost of debt financing.

Their findings also suggest that augmenting bank capital through higher bank earnings retention leads to increased bank loan rates. Additionally, these results indicate that if the banking system is weakly capitalised, there could be tensions between the monetary policy imperative of unlocking bank lending (expanding credit supply) and the supervisory objective of bank regulators (shrinking credit supply and ensuring resilience of banks).

Central banks have an important role in the liquidity creation process of an economy by controlling and monitoring the volume of money and credit available to the economy through monetary policy and other macroprudential tools. The relationship between liquidity creation and regulatory capital requirements have been investigated by various scholars. Acharya et al. (2020) examined the transmission of central bank liquidity to bank deposits and loan spreads in Europe between January 2006 and June 2010. The study found that central bank liquidity does not lead to a reduction of loan spreads for long maturity debts (more than one year) from high-risk banks. This is due to the fact that increasing bank capital, while at the same time easing monetary policy, can disrupt the effectiveness of the lending channel.

Furthermore, Casu et al. (2019) studied the link between regulatory capital requirements and liquidity creation after the implementation of Basel III. The study showed that banks may reduce liquidity creation as a response to an increase of capital requirements. Liquidity creation increases when banks decrease their capital ratios. These results indicate that there is a trade-off between financial stability, which is obtained by higher capital requirements (reduced risk) and economic growth driven by liquidity creation.

Comparable results were obtained by El-Massah et al. (2019) who used the generalised least squares model to estimate the determinants of liquidity risk in banks between 2009 and 2016. The results showed that capital adequacy has a positive impact on the liquidity risk of banks. These findings indicate that increasing bank capital requirements has a controlling impact on liquidity creation, and therefore leads to a decreased liquidity risk. Lower liquidity risk reduced liquidity creation, which ultimately leads to lower lending growth. These findings confirmed the results of Ben Naceur et al. (2018) who analysed the impact of increased bank capital requirements and liquidity on bank lending growth after the financial crisis of 2008. The results showed a negative correlation between capital ratios and bank lending growth for large European banks.

Contrarily to other scholars, results of studies published by Abbas et al. (2020) showed that there is a positive relationship between bank CAR and bank liquidity for medium-sized banks and a negative relationship between both variables is only confirmed for large commercial banks. These findings indicate that the correlation between bank capital regulations and bank liquidity is dependent on bank size. Furthermore, Igan and Mirzaei (2020) studied the cross-country differences in bank liquidity and capital levels and showed that banks with higher liquidity and capital ratios performed very well during times of crisis. However, there is only a marginal relationship between capital regulations and bank liquidity in pre-crisis times. Nevertheless, Jordà et al. (2021) observed that countries with a resilient capitalised bank system perform better during times of financial crisis.

Our study focused on the Canadian commercial and development banking, trading, and investment banking sector, as it is the main driver of Canadian bank loan to the non-financial sector, which ultimately supports the real economy. We adapted pre-existing models applied in previous studies published by other scholars such as Benetton et al. (2021), Gambacorta and Shin (2018), Glancy and Kurtzman (2018), Juelsrud and Wold (2020), Brei and Moreno (2019), and Imbierowicz et al. (2021).

Firstly, the results indicate that increases in regulatory capital requirements and consumer price index led to downward and upward changes in loan interest rate, respectively. These results had p values higher than 0.05, which means that the observed relationship is not statistically significant (Table 2.10). An effect size test confirmed the aforementioned results (Table 2.4). The eta-squared estimates of the effect size test (Table 2.4) indicate that the change in regulatory capital requirements explains only 0.25% of the observed variation. Similarly, the eta-squared estimates of the effect size test (Table 2.4) indicate that the Consumer Price Index variable explains only 0.02% of the observed variation. Hence, our results confirm that changes in regulatory capital requirements did not have a direct effect on the interest rates charged on loans offered by Canadian banks to the non-financial sector, over the period of 2012 to 2021.

The period of 2012 to 2021 was marked by economic growth and expansion, after the subprime crisis of 2008. Our results are in alignment with findings from previous studies conducted by Brei and Moreno (2019) who found that increases in regulatory capital requirements did not have an effect on loan interest rates during normal economic times. However, Brei and Moreno (2019) found that increases in regulatory capital requirement led to increases in loan interest rates during periods of large capital inflows.

Secondly, we observed that increases in return on assets by 1% over the previous year led to increases in loan interest rate by 0.70%, following increases in regulatory capital requirements (Table 2.10). This result was found to be statistically significant, with a p value lower than 0.05. The results suggest that Canadian banks obtain increased return on assets by boosting their profit margin through increases in loan interest rates, following increases in regulatory capital requirements (Table 2.10).

Thirdly, our results indicated that increases in bank size by 1% over the previous year led to a decrease in loan interest rate by 0.30%, following increases in regulatory capital requirements (Table 2.10). Furthermore, our results found that increases in liquidity levels over the previous year by 1% led to a decrease in loan interest rate by 0.01%, following increases in regulatory capital requirements (Table 2.10). The results were found to be statistically significant, with *p* values lower than 0.05. These results suggest that Canadian banks with increasing levels of liquidity and bank size (assets) are more likely to hold or decrease the level of their interest rates on lending facilities extended to the non-financial sector, following increases in regulatory capital requirements. This indicates that the effect of regulatory capital requirements on bank lending interest rate is indirectly controlled by Canadian banks' levels of liquidity and size. The results align with the findings of previous studies led by Abbas et al. (2020), Igan and Mirzaei (2020), and Jordà et al. (2021).

Fourthly, our study found that increases in regulatory capital requirements did not have a direct impact on the interest rates charged by Canadian banks, over the period of 2012 to 2021 (Table 2.10). The period of 2012 to 2021 corresponds to the economic growth and expansion time, after the subprime crisis of 2008. These results confirmed that increases in regulatory capital requirements did not have an effect on the loan interest rates of Canadian banks during normal economic times, characterised with economic growth and expansion. These findings confirmed the results of Brei and Moreno (2019).

Overall, our studies are consistent with previous literature and contribute to the scarce literature on the impact of regulatory capital requirements on banks' lending interest rates. Our results also offer regulators and policymakers with a set of recommendations.

Our study recommends that while regulators and policymakers should increase bank capital requirements during normal economic times to ensure Canadian banks have adequate reserves, they should also use increases in regulatory capital requirements as a key policy tool during times of large capital inflows to deal with asset depreciation and other macroeconomic issues caused by the expansion of aggregate demand and inflationary pressure.

Furthermore, we recommend that regulators and policymakers design and implement additional microprudential and supervisory tools with the objective of ensuring that banks do not use a profit margin-boosting mechanism, consisting of incrementing their lending interest rates, as the main path to meeting regulatory capital requirements.

Additionally, regulators and policymakers should require that banks set aside capital reserve requirements based on a combination of capital base increases, reduction of bank balance sheet risk, and sales of bank assets. This combination will ensure bank capital reserves are adequately diversified and resilient, leading to a more resilient banking industry.

Finally, the OSFI[1] requires banks that are designated as D-SIBs to maintain a CET1 surcharge of 1% of RWAs. Based on the results of our studies, we recommend that OSFI keeps these measures to ensure that large banks maintain additional reserves to account for the supplementary risk engendered by their size.

The remainder parts of this study are structured as follows: Section 3.2 provides details of research questions and hypotheses, Section 3.3 provides details on our sample data and variables, Section 3.4 presents empirical studies, Section 3.5 provides details of robustness checks, and Section 3.6 presents conclusions.

3.2 Research Questions and Hypotheses

The literature review presented in the previous section revealed the existence of mixed results regarding the implications of changes in banks' regulatory capital requirements on banks' lending behaviour.

Furthermore, the literature review also revealed that there were no studies regarding the impact of regulatory capital requirements on the lending volume and rate of Canadian banks. The conclusions of the literature review led to the following research question:

- **Research Question 2:** *What is the impact of banks' regulatory capital requirements on the Lending Rates of Canadian banks?*

Figure 3.1 presents a summary of the second research question and relevant hypothesis.

[1] Office of the Superintendent of Financial Institutions, Domestic Systemically Important Bank (D-SIB) Surcharge. Available from https://www.osfi-bsif.gc.ca/Eng/fi-if/rg-ro/gdn-ort/gl-ld/Pages/CAR22_chpt1.aspx#ToC1.8. November 2022.

Figure 1: Summary of Research Question 2		
Gap in Literature	**Research Question**	**Hypothesis**
▪ Mixed results regarding the implications of changes in banks' regulatory capital requirements on banks' lending behaviour. ▪ Limited literature regarding the impact of regulatory capital on lending volume and rates of Canadian banks.	What is the impact of banks' regulatory capital requirements on the Lending Rates of Canadian banks?	**H0**: Increase in banks' regulatory capital requirements **leads to a decrease** of Canadian banks' lending rate. **H1**: Increase in banks' regulatory capital requirements **leads to an increase** of Canadian banks lending rate. **H2**: Increase in banks' regulatory capital requirements **leads to no impact** on Canadian banks lending rate.

Fig. 3.1 Summary of research question 2

3.3 Data and Variables

This study uses the annual financial statistics of Canadian financial institutions from 2012 to 2021, from Fitch Connect database.[2] The aggregate total asset value of the entire Canadian banking industry over the period of 2012 to 2021 is 5.2 trillion USD. Universal Commercial Banks, Wholesale Commercial Banks, Development Banks, Investment and Trading Banks hold 4.8 trillion USD in aggregate total assets, over the same period. Our sample covers Universal Commercial Banks, Wholesale Commercial Banks, Development Banks, and Investment and Trading Banks, representing 120 Canadian banks, and accounting for 92% of the Canadian banking sector, in terms of aggregate total assets over the period of 2012 to 2021. Our sample also covers Monetary Policy Rates and Inflation Rates data from the Bank of Canada,[3] from 2012 and 2021.

Our study focuses on the Canadian commercial, development, investment, and trading banking sector, given that it is the main vehicle of lending to the non-financial sector, which supports the real economy. Contrarily to the financial economy, which covers transactions of money and financial assets, the real economy is more connected to economic growth and encompasses the production and distribution of goods and

[2] Fitch Solutions, Canadian Bank Financials Data, from 2012 to 2021. Available from Fitch Solutions. July 2022.

[3] Bank of Canada, Overnight Rate and Inflation – Control Target, from 2012 to 2021. Available from Bank of Canada. November 2022.

services. Furthermore, corporate loans to the non-financial sector tend to have shorter debt maturities, aligning more with changes in regulatory capital requirements.

The study investigated the impact of changes in regulatory capital requirements on the loan interest rates charged by Canadian banks. We measure the loan interest rates charged by Canadian banks, by dividing the Interest Income on Loans over the Average Gross Loans offered by Canadian banks.

The introduction of Basel III in 2010 required banks to maintain a minimum CAR of 8%, which is determined considering Tier 1 capital and Tier 2 capital only, eliminating Tier 3 capital from the CAR calculation.[4]

The OSFI[5] defines total regulatory capital as Tier 1 regulatory capital plus Tier 2 capital. Tier 1 regulatory capital is the aggregation of Common Equity Tier 1 (CET1) capital and Additional Tier 1 capital.

OSFI[6] defines Tier 2 capital (prior to regulatory adjustments) as the sum of the following items: Instruments issued by the financial institution that meet the criteria for inclusion in Tier 2 capital (and are not included in Tier 1 capital); surplus (share premium) emanating from the issue of instruments included in Tier 2 capital; instruments issued by consolidated subsidiaries of the financial institution and held by third parties that meet the criteria for inclusion in Tier 2 capital (and are not included in Tier 1 capital); and certain loan loss allowances that meet the criteria for inclusion in Tier 2 capital.

OSFI[7] defines Total regulatory capital requirements (Total Reg Cap Ratio) as the sum of risk-based capital ratios, conservation buffer, and a countercyclical buffer (where applicable). Risk-based capital ratios are calculated by dividing total capital (Total Reg Cap) by the sum of credit, operational, and market RWAs. OSFI requires Canadian banks to maintain

[4] Basel Committee on Banking Supervision, History of the Basel Committee (Basel III: Responding to the 2007–09 Financial Crisis). Available from https://www.bis.org/bcbs/history.htm. April 2022.

[5] Office of the Superintendent of Financial Institutions, Requirements for Inclusion in Regulatory Capital. Available from https://www.osfi-bsif.gc.ca/en/guidance/guidance-library/capital-adequacy-requirements-car-2024-chapter-2-definition-capital. July 2022.

[6] Office of the Superintendent of Financial Institutions, Tier 2 Capital. Available from https://www.osfi-bsif.gc.ca/en/guidance/guidance-library/capital-adequacy-requirements-car-2024-chapter-2-definition-capital. July 2022.

[7] Office of the Superintendent of Financial Institutions, Calculation of OSFI Minimum Capital Requirements. Available from https://www.osfi-bsif.gc.ca/Eng/fi-if/rg-ro/gdn-ort/gl-ld/Pages/CAR22_chpt1.aspx. July 2022.

a minimum capital requirement ratio, in addition to a conservation buffer (where applicable), a countercyclical buffer (where applicable), and Basel III leverage ratio.

Canadian banks are regulated by the OSFI and are required to abide by regulatory capital requirements set by OSFI. Our study used the annual variation in (Total regulatory capital ratios + Basel III leverage ratios) disclosed to OSFI by Canadian banks, as part of their annual financial disclosure.

$$\Delta \text{ in Total Reg Cap Ratio} = \Delta \text{ in} \frac{\text{Total Reg Cap}}{\text{RWA}} + \Delta \text{ in Basel III Leverage Ratio}$$

We used lagged values of Return on Assets, Bank Size, and Ratio of Core Deposits as control variables to account for bank effects.

The lagged values of Return on Assets and Ratio of Liquid Assets to Total Assets were calculated using the values of Return on Assets and Ratio of Liquid Assets to Total Assets, disclosed by the Canadian bank in the previous year (t–1).

The lagged value of Bank Size is the lagged value of the logarithm of Total Assets.

The lagged value of the Ratio of Core Deposits was obtained by using the lagged Ratio of Total Customer Deposits to Total Assets.

Variables measuring Monetary Policy Rate and Inflation Rate were introduced to control for macroeconomic effects.

Inflation Rate is measured by the yearly average of Canadian consumer price index, from the Bank of Canada.

Monetary Policy Rate is measured by the yearly average of the Overnight Target Rate, from the Bank of Canada.

A fixed effect model (Panel Data Regression) enables the control for all time-invariant differences between observed entities. This ensures that the coefficients of the time effect model are not biased due to the non-inclusion or omission of time-invariant characteristics of the entity.

In the case of our research, the time-invariant characteristics could be the bank's corporate culture, bank's internal policy, and bank's management strategy.

However, time-invariant characteristics such as bank's corporate culture, bank's internal policy, and bank's management strategy could also be classified as time-variant characteristics. Bank's corporate culture, bank's internal policy, and bank's management strategy could be modified multiple times during a year.

In the empirical study, we included bank control variables which are the results of the bank's corporate culture, bank's internal policy, and bank's management strategy.

In the empirical study of the impact of changes in regulatory capital requirements on the loan interest rates charged by Canadian banks, the bank control variables account for lagged values of Return on Assets, Bank Size, and Ratio of Core Deposits.

The values of the bank control variables incorporate the effect of banks' internal characteristics. Therefore, the incorporation of the bank control variables in the multiple regression controls for effects of banks' internal characteristics. Furthermore, given that the differences between the banks (entities) are correlated with predictors (bank control variables), a random effect model (Panel Model Regression) does not emerge as an option.

Komath et al. (2023) studied the impact of corporate governance and related controversies on the market value of banks. The results of their study found that there is a statistically significant relationship between the corporate governance controversies scores and the market value of banks.

Barth and Mansouri (2021) studied the role of corporate culture in banking. The authors found that corporate culture is a softer aspect of governance necessary to enhance banking stability. Specifically, they found that banks with a more pronounced competition-oriented culture have stronger bonus-focused compensation schemes. Banks with a strong focus on growth demonstrated higher stock returns, and finally, banks with a focus on stability had lower bankruptcy risk.

Table 3.1 presents a summarised description of variables.

The statistics on the interest rates on Loans offered by Canadian banks to the non-financial sector showed some spurious outliers. Hence, we transformed the statistics through winsorisation to limit the effect of extreme values or spurious outliers.

Table 3.2 presents descriptive statistics following winsorisation.

Table 3.2 (Descriptive Statistics) shows that the interest rates on loans offered by Canadian banks to the non-financial sector is 4.00% on average, while the yearly change in regulatory capital requirements is 2.28% on average.

Table 3.3 presents the annual average change in regulatory capital requirements and the annual average change in Canadian banks' interest rate on loans to the non-financial sector, following winsorisation.

Table 3.1 Description of variables

	Definition	*Data Source*
Dependent Variable		
Loan Interest Rate	Interest Income on Loans divided by Average Gross Loans (%).	Fitch Connect Database
Independent Variable		
Annual Δ Canadian Bank Capital Requirements	Annual variation in (Total regulatory capital ratios + Basel III leverage ratios) disclosed to OSFI by Canadian banks, as part of their annual financial disclosure. We adopted a conservative approach for the calculation of Lagged (t–1) Excess capital by utilising the most stringent minimum capital requirement.	Fitch Connect Database
Bank Control Variables		
Lagged (t–1) Return on Assets	Lagged Return on Assets	Fitch Connect Database
Lagged (t–1) Bank Size	Lagged Logarithm of Total Assets	Fitch Connect Database
Lagged (t–1) Ratio of Core Deposit	Lagged Ratio of Total Core Deposits (Total Customer Deposits) to Total Assets.	Fitch Connect Database
Macroeconomic Control Variables		
Inflation CPI	Yearly Average Inflation CPI	Bank of Canada
Monetary Policy (Overnight Target Rate)	Yearly Average Overnight Target Rate	Bank of Canada

The observation of the annual average change in regulatory capital requirements and the annual average change in Canadian banks' interest rates on gross loan to the non-financial sector, following winsorisation (Table 3.3) do not lead to a specific conclusion regarding the impact of regulatory capital requirements on the interest rates charged by banks. Further analysis is necessary to ascertain the true impact of regulatory capital requirements on Canadian banks' interest rates on gross loan to the non-financial sector. The subsequent pages will provide a detailed empirical analysis.

Table 3.2 Descriptive statistics

	Mean	*Standard Deviation*
Dependent Variable		
Loan Interest Rate	4.00	1.29
Independent Variable		
Annual Δ Canadian Bank Capital Requirements	2.28	12.90
Bank Control Variables		
Lagged (t–1) Return on Assets	0.57	0.84
Lagged (t–1) Bank Size	3.53	1.04
Lagged (t–1) Ratio of Core Deposit	64.13	26.78
Macroeconomic Control Variables		
Inflation CPI	1.68	0.72
Monetary Policy (Overnight Target Rate)	0.87	0.43
Observations		255

Note: Shown are the descriptive statistics using financial statistics of Canadian financial institutions and macroeconomic data, from 2012 to 2021, for variables described in Table 3.1.

Table 3.3 Annual average of changes in regulatory capital requirements and Canadian banks' interest rates

Year	*Mean of Annual Δ Canadian Bank Capital Requirements*	*Mean of Annual Δ Bank Loan Interest Rate*
2012	–	–
2013	12.51	–3.26
2014	11.40	–1.35
2015	2.89	-12.91
2016	3.2	10.50
2017	1.70	16.22
2018	–0.69	13.12
2019	3.62	18.59
2020	2.22	–1.40
2021	2.72	–1.01

Note: Shown are the annual average changes in regulatory capital requirements and the annual average changes in Canadian banks' interest rate on loans to the non-financial sector, following winsorisation.

3.4 Results

We analysed the effect of changes in regulatory capital requirements on the interest rates charged on loans offered by Canadian banks to the non-financial sector. Our empirical studies adapted pre-existing models, previously applied by other researchers such as Benetton et al. (2021), Gambacorta and Shin (2018), Glancy and Kurtzman (2018), Juelsrud and Wold (2020), Brei and Moreno (2019), and Imbierowicz et al. (2021), for the study of changes in capital requirements and interest rates on lending in other jurisdictions, other than Canada.

The adaptation of pre-existing models ensures our studies follow a scientific rigour and enables the comparison of our results with those of previous studies. Our model is also the result of the application of econometric methods and principles from Gourieroux and Jasiak (2018), Campbell et al. (1996), as well as research methods recommendations from Chevalier et al. (2019).

Additionally, our model is also the result of the application of knowledge acquired through the literature review, as well as professional and managerial experiences. The validity and goodness-of-fit of our model is demonstrated through the model statistics, regression assumption tests and robustness tests presented in subsequent sections.

Adapting pre-existing regression models used by Brei and Moreno (2019), Benetton et al. (2021), Gambacorta and Shin (2018), Glancy and Kurtzman (2018), Juelsrud and Wold (2020), and Imbierowicz et al. (2021), we studied the transmission of changes of Canadian regulatory capital requirements to the interest rates charged by Canadian banks on loans offered to the non-financial sector, applying the following multiple regression model:

$$\mathbf{Y}_{\mathbf{a,t}} = \propto_0 + \sum_{t=1}^{t=10} \alpha_{1.t}\Delta\mathbf{Cap}_{\mathbf{a,t}} + \beta\mathbf{X}_{\mathbf{a,t-1}} + f_a + \varepsilon_{a,t} \qquad \text{(Model 2)}$$

where:

$\Delta\mathbf{Y}_{\mathbf{a,t}}$ is the Interest Rate charged by Canadian bank 'a' in year 't'. It is obtained through dividing the Interest Income by Average Gross Loans.

$\Delta\mathbf{Cap}_{\mathbf{a,t}}$ is the change in Regulatory bank capital requirement ratio for bank 'a', during year 't'. $\Delta\mathbf{Cap}_{\mathbf{a,t}}$ is calculated using the annual variation in (Total regulatory capital ratios + Basel III leverage ratios) disclosed to OSFI by Canadian banks, as part of their annual financial disclosure.

$$\Delta \text{ in Total Reg Cap Ratio} = \Delta \text{ in} \frac{\text{Total Reg Cap}}{\text{RWA}} + \Delta \text{ in Basel III Leverage Ratio}$$

We introduced a vector of lagged bank-specific variables to control for bank effects. $\mathbf{X}_{\mathbf{a,t-1}}$ represents a vector of lagged bank-specific control variables, capturing the Return on Assets, Bank Size, and Ratio of core Deposits to Total Assets.

The lagged values of Return on Assets and Ratio of Liquid Assets to Total Assets were calculated using the values of Return on Assets and Ratio of Liquid Assets to Total Assets, disclosed by the Canadian bank in the previous year (t–1).

The lagged value of Bank Size is the lagged value of the logarithm of Total Assets.

The lagged value of the Ratio of Core Deposits was obtained by using the lagged Ratio of Total Customer Deposits to Total Assets.

f_a is the vector of macroeconomic control variables introduced to control for macroeconomic effects. Variables measuring Inflation Rate (CPI), and Central Bank Policy Rate were introduced to control for macroeconomic effects.

Table 3.4 presents the results of the multiple regression analysing the effect of the changes in regulatory capital requirements on the interest rates charged on loans offered by Canadian banks to the non-financial sector.

We verified the strength of the relationship between the dependent variable (Interest Rate) and independent variables, by performing an effect size test.

Table 3.5 presents the results of the effect size test.

We also tested regression assumptions supporting our multiple regression model. Table 3.6 presents the results of the Shapiro–Wilk W test for normal data.

The *p* value of the Shapiro–Wilk W test (*p* value of 0.00) confirmed that r is not normally distributed. Therefore, we conducted a non-parametric test (Kruskal–Wallis) to control for non-normality. Table 3.7 presents the results of the Kruskal–Wallis equality-of-populations rank test.

The *p* value (>0.05) of the Kruskal–Wallis equality-of-populations rank test is 0.67. Therefore, the null hypothesis is accepted, and we can confirm that the yearly Change in Canadian Bank loan's interest rate and yearly Change in total bank capital requirement ratios follow the same statistical distribution.

Table 3.8 presents the results of the test of autocorrelation (Breusch–Godfrey LM Test for autocorrelation).

The *p* value (<0.05) of the Breusch–Godfrey LM test is 0.0084. Therefore, the null hypothesis is rejected, and we can confirm that there is serial correlation (autocorrelation). The multiple regression estimates assume that the observations are independent, meaning they are not

Table 3.4 Impact of changes in bank regulatory capital requirements on the loan interest rates charged by Canadian banks (multiple regression)

	Interest Rate
Independent Variable	
Annual Δ Canadian Bank Capital Requirements Ratio	–0.004 (0.42)
Bank Control Variables	
Lagged (t–1) Return on Assets	**0.70 (0.00)*****
Lagged (t–1) Bank Size	**–0.30 (0.00)*****
Lagged (t–1) Ratio of Core Deposits	**–0.017 (0.00)*****
Macroeconomic Control Variables	
Inflation Rate (CPI)	0.02 (0.83)
Central Bank Policy Rate	**0.43 (0.00)*****
Other Details	
Observations	255
Number of banks	120
R^2	0.3307
Prob > F	0.0000

Note: Shown are the results of the multiple regression analysis using the multiple regression model presented above. The statistical significance of results is indicated by *10% level, **5% level and ***1% level using standard errors. *p* values are presented in parentheses after coefficient estimates.

Table 3.5 Effect size test

	Eta-Squared	*df*	*95% conf. interval*
Independent Variable			
Model	0.33	6	0.22–0.40
Annual Δ Canadian Bank Capital Requirements Ratio	0.0025	1	0.00–0.03
Bank Control Variables			
Lagged (t–1) Return on Assets	0.16	1	0.08–0.24
Lagged (t–1) Bank Size	0.07	1	0.02–0.14
Lagged (t– Ratio of Core Deposits	0.10	1	0.04–0.18
Macroeconomic Control Variables			
Inflation Rate (CPI)	0.00018	1	0.00–0.015
Central Bank Policy Rate	0.04434	1	0.00–0.10

correlated. The presence of autocorrelation indicates that there is a level of correlation between the variables of the same observations. Therefore, we re-estimated the initial model, introducing robust standards errors to correct the effects of autocorrelation.

Table 3.9 presents the results of the test of multicollinearity.

We tested for multicollinearity using the VIF, which measures the value of multicollinearity amongst regression variables. The test found a VIF value of 1.06 (<10), indicating that there is no multicollinearity.

Table 3.10 presents the results of the test of homoscedasticity of residuals (Breusch–Pagan/Cook–Weisberg test for heteroscedasticity).

The p value of the Cameron & Trivedi's decomposition of IM test, and White's test for heteroscedasticity is 0.00. Therefore, the null hypothesis is rejected, and we can confirm that the variance of residuals is not

Table 3.6 Shapiro–Wilk W test for normal data

Variable	*Obs*	*W*	*V*	*Z*	*Prob>z*
R	255	0.96660	6.164	4.235	0.00001

Table 3.7 Non-parametric test to control for non-normality (Kruskal–Wallis equality-of-populations rank test)

Chi2	*Prob*
Chi2 (225) = 215.01	0.67
Chi2 (225) with ties = 215.10	0.67

Note: Kruskal–Wallis equality-of-populations rank test for Loan Interest Rates and yearly change in total bank capital requirement ratio.

Table 3.8 Test of autocorrelation (Breusch–Godfrey LM test)

lags(p)	*chi2*	*df*	*Prob > chi2*
1	6.936	1	0.0084

Table 3.9 Test of multicollinearity (VIF)

Results - Test of Multicollinearity
Mean VIF = 1.06

Table 3.10 Test of homoscedasticity of residuals (Cameron & Trivedi's decomposition of IM test & White's test)

	chi2	*df*	*p*
Cameron & Trivedi's Decomposition of IM Test			
Heteroscedasticity	117.61	34	0.00
White's Test			
H0: Homoscedasticity	chi2(27) = 104.48		
Ha: Unrestricted heteroscedasticity	Prob > chi2 = 0.00		

homogenous (heteroscedasticity). The presence of heteroscedasticity could be due subpopulation differences, model misspecifications, or measurement errors. Therefore, we re-estimated the initial model, introducing robust standards errors to correct the effects of heteroscedasticity.

Table 3.11 presents the results of the multiple regression analysing the effect of the changes in regulatory capital requirements on the interest rates charged on loans offered by Canadian banks to the non-financial sector, with the introduction of robust standard errors.

The *p* values related to the robust standard errors (Table 3.11) are different to the *p* values related to the standard errors obtained in the initial model estimation (Table 3.4). The issues of heteroscedasticity and serial correlation (autocorrelation) have been resolved, with the introduction of robust standard errors.

Firstly, while the results indicate that increases in regulatory capital requirements, and consumer price index led to negative and positive changes in loan interest rate respectively, these results had *p* values higher than 0.05, which indicates that the observed relationship is not statistically significant (Table 3.11).

An effect size test confirmed the aforementioned results (Table 3.4). The eta-squared estimates of the effect size test (Table 3.4) indicate that the change in regulatory capital requirements explains only 0.25% of the observed variation. Therefore, our results confirm that changes in regulatory capital requirements did not have a direct impact on the interest rates charged on loans offered by Canadian banks to the non-financial sector, over the period of 2012 to 2021.

The period of 2012 to 2021 was characterised by economic growth and expansion, post the financial crisis of 2008. The empirical results of our study are consistent with findings from previous studies led by Brei and Moreno (2019). They found that increases in regulatory capital requirements did not impact loan interest rates during normal economic times. However, Brei and Moreno (2019) found that increases in regulatory capital requirement led to increases loan interest rates during periods of large capital inflows.

Secondly, the study found that increases in return on assets by 1% led to increases in loan interest rate by 0.70%, following increases in regulatory capital requirements (Table 3.11). This result was statistically significant, with a *p* value lower than 0.05. The results suggest that Canadian banks obtain increased return on assets by boosting their profit margin through increases in loan interest rates, following increases in regulatory capital requirements (Table 3.11).

Table 3.11 Impact of changes in bank regulatory capital requirements on the loan interest rate of Canadian banks, with the introduction of robust standard errors

	Interest Rate
Independent Variable	
Annual Δ Canadian Bank Capital Requirements Ratio	–0.004 (0.57)
Bank Control Variables	
Lagged (t–1) Return on Assets	**0.70 (0.000)*** **
Lagged (t–1) Bank Size	**–0.30 (0.000)*** **
Lagged (t–1) Ratio of Core Deposits	**–0.01 (0.000)*** **
Macroeconomic Control Variables	
Inflation Rate (CPI)	0.01 (0.85)
Central Bank Policy Rate	**0.43 (0.001)*** **
Other Details	
Observations	255
Number of banks	120
R^2	0.3307
Prob > F	0.0000

Note: Shown are the results of the multiple regression analysis using the multiple regression model presented above, and introducing robust standard errors. The statistical significance of results is indicated by *10% level, **5% level and ***1% level using robust standard errors. *p* values are presented in parentheses after coefficient estimates.

Thirdly, our results found that increases in bank size by 1% led to a decrease in loan interest rate by 0.30%, following increases in regulatory capital requirements (Table 3.11). Furthermore, our results found that increases in liquidity levels (Ratio of Core Deposits) by 1% led to a decrease in loan interest rate by 0.01%, following increases in regulatory capital requirements (Table 3.11). The results were statistically significant, with p values lower than 0.05.

These results suggest that Canadian banks with incremental levels of liquidity and bank size (assets) are more likely to maintain or decrease the level of their interest rates on loans offered to the non-financial sector, following increases in regulatory capital requirements. This indicates that the impact of regulatory capital requirements on banks' lending rate is indirectly controlled by Canadian banks' levels of liquidity and size.

The results also suggest that Canadian banks that are able to increase their levels of liquidity and bank size (assets) are more likely to perform well during times of crisis, given their higher levels of reserves in liquidity and assets.

The results are in line with Abbas et al. (2020), Igan and Mirzaei (2020), and Jordà et al. (2021). Abbas et al. (2020) found that the correlation between bank capital regulations and bank liquidity is dependent on bank size. Igan and Mirzaei (2020) studied the cross-country differences in bank liquidity and capital levels and found that banks with higher liquidity and capital ratios performed very well during times of crisis. This was confirmed by Jordà et al. (2021) who found that countries with strongly capitalised banking systems perform better during times of financial crisis.

The multiple regression coefficients found that increasing regulatory capital requirements did not have a direct effect on the interest rates charged by Canadian banks, over the period of 2012 to 2021, which corresponds to the economic growth and expansion time, post the subprime crisis of 2008 (Table 3.11).

These results confirmed that increases in regulatory capital requirements did not impact loan interest rates during normal economic times, characterised with economic growth and expansion. These findings confirmed the results of Brei and Moreno (2019) who found that increases in regulatory capital requirements only led to increases in loan interest rates during times of large capital inflows, and not during normal economic times.

Times of large capital inflows are normally characterised by credit booms, significant expansion of aggregate demand and inflationary pressure. While regulators and policymakers should increase bank capital requirements during normal economic times to ensure Canadian banks have adequate reserves, they should also:

- Use increases in regulatory capital requirements *as a key policy tool during times of large capital inflows* to *deal with asset depreciation and other macroeconomic issues* caused by the expansion of aggregate demand and inflationary pressure.

Furthermore, the multiple regression coefficients found that, Canadian banks obtain increased return on assets by boosting their profit margin through increases in loan interest rates, following increases in regulatory capital requirements. Therefore, regulators and policymakers should:

- Design and implement *additional microprudential and supervisory tools* aimed at ensuring that *banks do not use a profit margin-boosting mechanism*, consisting of increasing loan interest rates, as the main avenue for meeting regulatory capital requirements.

This means that regulators and policymakers should require that banks build their capital reserve requirements using a combination of capital base increases, reduction of bank balance sheet risk, and sales of bank assets. This will ensure bank capital reserves are adequately diversified and resilient, leading to a more resilient banking industry.

Additionally, the multiple regression coefficients found that, Canadian banks with increasing levels of liquidity and bank size (assets) are more likely to maintain or decrease the level of the interest rates on loans that they offer to the non-financial sector, following increases in regulatory capital requirements. This suggests that the impact of regulatory capital requirements on bank lending rate is indirectly controlled by Canadian banks' levels of liquidity and size. Therefore, bank regulators and policymakers should:

- Ensure that *banks with high levels of liquidity* and *size* build *additional reserves* in the form of *risk-based surcharges.*

The OSFI,[8] which is the regulator of the Canadian banking sector requires banks that are designated as D-SIBs to maintain a CET1 surcharge of 1% of RWAs. We recommend that OSFI keeps these measures to ensure that large banks maintain additional reserves to account for the supplementary risk engendered by their size.

[8] Office of the Superintendent of Financial Institutions, Domestic Systemically Important Bank (D-SIB) Surcharge. Available from https://www.osfi-bsif.gc.ca/Eng/fi-if/rg-ro/gdn-ort/gl-ld/Pages/CAR22_chpt1.aspx#ToC1.8. November 2022.

3.5 Robustness Tests

We performed a series of the robustness checks to assess for the sensitivity of our results to changes in variables, model composition, and sample. Hence, we re-performed the multiple regression model (Model 2, Table 3.4) using different subsamples. Firstly, we re-estimated the multiple regression model, excluding bank control variables.

Table 3.12 presents the results of the robustness check, evaluating the impact of changes in bank regulatory capital requirements on the loan interest rates charged by Canadian banks, excluding bank control variables.

The results (Table 3.12) of the robustness check evaluating the impact of changes in bank regulatory capital requirements on the loan interest rate charged by Canadian banks align with those previously obtained through the initial estimation of the multiple regression model (Model 2, Table 3.4).

Table 3.12 Impact of changes in bank regulatory capital requirements on the interest rate of Canadian banks, excluding bank control variables

	Interest Rate
Independent Variable	
Annual Δ Canadian Bank Capital Requirements Ratio	–0.001 (0.84)
Bank Control Variables	
Lagged (t–1) Return on Assets	Excluded
Lagged (t–1) Bank Size	Excluded
Lagged (t–1) Ratio of Core Deposits	Excluded
Macroeconomic Control Variables	
Inflation Rate (CPI)	–0.01 (0.89)
Central Bank Policy Rate	**0.55** **(0.00)***
Other Details	
Observations	257
Number of banks	120
R^2	0.0483
Prob > F	0.0057

Note: The statistical significance of results is indicated by *10% level, **5% level and ***1% level using standard errors. *p* values are presented in parentheses after coefficient estimates.

Secondly, we re-estimated the multiple regression model, excluding macroeconomic control variables. Table 3.13 presents the results of the robustness check evaluating the impact of changes in bank regulatory capital requirements on the loan interest rate charged by Canadian banks, excluding macroeconomic control variables.

The results (Table 3.13) of the robustness check evaluating the impact of changes in bank regulatory capital requirements on the loan interest rate charged by Canadian banks, excluding macroeconomic control variables, align with those previously obtained through the initial estimation of the multiple regression model (Model 2, Table 3.4).

Thirdly, we re-estimated the multiple regression model, excluding bank control variables, and macroeconomic control variables. Table 3.14 presents the results of the robustness check evaluating the impact of changes in bank regulatory capital requirements on the loan interest rate charged

Table 3.13 Impact of changes in bank regulatory capital requirements on the interest rate of Canadian banks, excluding macroeconomic control variables

	Interest Rate
Independent Variable	
Annual Δ Canadian Bank Capital Requirements Ratio	–0.004 (0.41)
Bank Control Variables	
Lagged (t–1) Return on Assets	**0.73** **(0.000)*** **
Lagged (t–1) Bank Size	**–0.30** **(0.000)*** **
Lagged (t–1) Ratio of Core Deposits	**–0.01** **(0.000)*** **
Macroeconomic Control Variables	
Inflation Rate (CPI)	Excluded
Central Bank Policy Rate	Excluded
Other Details	
Observations	255
Number of banks	120
R^2	0.2991
Prob > F	0.0000

Note: The statistical significance of results is indicated by *10% level, **5% level and ***1% level using standard errors. *p* values are presented in parentheses after coefficient estimates.

Table 3.14 Impact of changes in bank regulatory capital requirements on the loan interest rate of Canadian banks, excluding bank control effect and macroeconomic control variables

	Interest Rate
Independent Variable	
Annual Δ Canadian Bank Capital Requirements Ratio	–0.001 (0.84)
Bank Control Variables	
Lagged (t–1) Return on Assets	Excluded
Lagged (t–1) Bank Size	Excluded
Lagged (t–1) Ratio of Core Deposits	Excluded
Macroeconomic Control Variables	
Inflation Rate (CPI)	Excluded
Central Bank Policy Rate	Excluded
Other Details	
Observations	257
Number of banks	120
R^2	0.0002
Prob > F	0.8419

Note: The statistical significance of results is indicated by *10% level, **5% level and ***1% level using standard errors. *p* values are presented in parentheses after coefficient estimates.

by Canadian banks, excluding bank control variables, and macroeconomic control variables.

The results (Table 3.14) of the robustness check evaluating the impact of changes in bank regulatory capital requirements on the loan interest rate charged by Canadian banks, excluding bank control effect and macroeconomic control variables, align with those previously obtained through the initial estimation of the multiple regression model (Model 2, Table 3.4).

3.6 Conclusion and Managerial Recommendation

This study analysed the effect of changes in regulatory capital requirements on the interest rates charged on loans offered by Canadian banks to the non-financial sector.

The results noted that increases in regulatory capital requirements did not impact loan interest rates during normal economic times, characterised with economic growth and expansion. These findings confirmed the results of Brei and Moreno (2019) who found that increases in regulatory capital requirements only led to increases in loan interest rates during times of large capital inflows, and not during normal economic times. Times of large capital inflows are normally characterised by credit booms, significant expansion of aggregate demand and inflationary pressure. These results confirm that hypotheses H0 and H1 were rejected, in favour of hypothesis H2. H0, H1 and H2 are described in Section 3.3 above.

Overall, our studies are in line with previous literature and contribute to the scarce literature on the impact of regulatory capital requirements on banks' lending interest rates. Our results also offer regulators and policymakers with a set of recommendations, aiming at ensuring that increases in regulatory capital requirements do not lead to severe increases in lending interest rates on loans to the non-financial sector, which could reduce the volume of liquidity available to the non-financial sector, and negatively impact recovery efforts targeting the consequences of an economic downturn.

Our study recommends that while regulators and policymakers increase bank capital requirements during normal economic times to ensure Canadian banks have adequate reserves, they should also use increases in regulatory capital requirements as a key policy tool during times of large capital inflows to deal with asset depreciation and other macroeconomic issues caused by the expansion of aggregate demand and inflationary pressure.

Furthermore, the study found that Canadian banks obtain increased return on assets by boosting their profit margin through increases in loan interest rates, following increases in regulatory capital requirements. We recommend that regulators and policymakers design and implement additional microprudential and supervisory tools aimed at ensuring that banks do not use a profit margin-boosting mechanism, consisting of increasing loan interest rates, as the main avenue for meeting regulatory capital requirements. Additionally, regulators and policymakers should require that banks build their capital reserve requirements using a combination of capital base increases, reduction of bank balance sheet risk, and sales of bank assets. This will ensure bank capital reserves are adequately diversified and resilient, leading to a more resilient banking industry.

Our studies also found that Canadian banks with increasing levels of liquidity and bank size (assets) are more likely to maintain or decrease the level of their interest rates on loans offered to the non-financial sector, following increases in regulatory capital requirements. This suggests that the impact of regulatory capital requirements on bank lending rate is indirectly controlled by Canadian banks' levels of liquidity and size.

Bank regulators and policymakers should ensure that banks with high levels of liquidity and size build additional reserves in the form of risk-based surcharges. The OSFI[9] requires banks that are designated as D-SIBs to maintain a CET1 surcharge of 1% of RWAs. In alignment with our results, we recommend that OSFI keeps these measures to ensure that large banks maintain additional reserves to account for the supplementary risk engendered by their size. The Appendix provides a detailed summary of the managerial recommendations.

Our studies were limited by the existence of missed values, and a sample that only covered the period post-subprime crisis (2012 to 2021). Theoretically, we have 1200 observations (120 Canadian banks observed over 10 years). However, STATA only counts the number of observations for which there are values for all variables and years. Other limitations related to the presence of spurious outliers were mitigated by winsorising the samples utilised for the study of the research question.

Finally, future studies should investigate how banks' lending portfolio is impacted by increases in regulatory capital requirements.

Hence, Chapter 4 will analyse the impact of bank regulatory capital requirements on Canadian banks' gross loan portfolio.

[9] Office of the Superintendent of Financial Institutions, Domestic Systemically Important Bank (D-SIB) Surcharge. Available from https://www.osfi-bsif.gc.ca/Eng/fi-if/rg-ro/gdn-ort/gl-ld/Pages/CAR22_chpt1.aspx#ToC1.8. November 2022.

CHAPTER 4

Impact of Bank Regulatory Capital Requirements: On Canadian Banks' Gross Loan Portfolio

Abstract This chapter investigated the effect of changes in regulatory capital requirements on the components of the portfolio of gross loan offered by Canadian banks to the non-financial sector. The study covered the three largest components of the portfolio of gross loan offered by Canadian banks to the non-financial sector: Corporate & Commercial Loans (26% of Gross Loans), Residential Mortgage Loans (44% of Gross Loans), and Other Consumer/Retail Loans (20% of Gross Loans).

The study used a sample of annual financial statistics of Canadian financial institutions from 2012 to 2021, from Fitch Connect database, over the period of 2012 to 2021. The data also encompasses macroeconomic statistics from the Bank of Canada, BIS, and Economic Policy Uncertainty Research Group.

The results suggested that changes in Canadian regulatory bank capital requirement ratio had a direct downward impact on only the portion of Canadian lending portfolio that accounts for Corporate & Commercial Loans. The results also found that the impact of the increase in the Canadian regulatory bank capital requirements on Corporate & Commercial Loans is dependent on changes in economic policy.

B. Piper, *The Effect of Changes in Regulatory Capital Requirements on Banks Lending*
https://doi.org/10.1007/978-3-032-02208-0_4

Additionally, the study found that in times of economic policy uncertainty, Canadian banks with an increased return on assets over the previous year decreased their credit allocation towards Residential Mortgage Loans, following an increase in Canadian regulatory bank capital requirements. However, the level of credit portfolio allocation by Canadian banks to other Consumer/Retail Loans is rather impacted by the macroeconomic environment.

Keywords Basel Accords • Regulatory Capital Requirements • Canadian Bank Lending Portfolio • Canadian Bank Lending Behaviour • Macroprudential Regulations • Microprudential Regulations • GDP • Bank Size • Bank Liquidity • Monetary Policy, Inflation Rate (CPI) • GDP Gap • Business Climate • and Credit-to-GDP Gap

4.1 Introduction

In this chapter, we analysed the effect of changes in regulatory capital requirements on the portfolio of gross loan offered by Canadian banks to the non-financial sector. To this aim, we used a sample of annual financial statistics of Canadian financial institutions from 2012 to 2021, from Fitch Connect database, covering Universal Commercial Banks, Wholesale Commercial Banks, Development Banks, as well as Trading and Investment Banks, representing 120 Canadian banks, and accounting for more than 90% of the Canadian banking sector, in terms of aggregate total assets over the period of 2012 to 2021.

Bank regulatory capital reserve requirements represent a prudential tool used by financial regulators and policymakers to achieve financial stability and ensure that banks have sufficient capital reserves to remain resilient during times of economic crisis or downturn. While increases in bank regulatory capital requirements by financial regulators provide regulators and policymakers with tools aimed at stabilising the financial system, it does have adverse effects on the portfolio of Canadian banks' loans to the non-financial sector. This study aims at analysing the impact of changes in regulatory capital requirements on the components of the portfolio of loan offered by Canadian banks to the non-financial sector.

The financial crisis of 2008 demonstrated the limits of Basel I and II. The crisis highlighted that banks were overleveraged and undercapitalised. Following the financial crisis of 2008, the Basel Committee on Banking

Supervision designed and implemented the Third Basel Accord (Basel III) to strengthen the level and composition of capital reserves required from banks, while building upon the foundations of Basel I and II. The application of Basel III underscored the importance for regulators to ensure that banks have adequate reserves to withstand the effects of financial crises.

Previous empirical results from single-country studies found that in a recent study, DeYoung et al. (2018) studied the liquidity behaviour of banks in the USA that experience liquidity shocks impacting their equity capital ratios between 1998 and 2012. The results noted that US banks with assets less than $1 billion (unregulated) treated liquidity and (regulated) capital as substitutes, in response to exogeneous shocks to their regulatory capital ratios. The substitution effect translated into banks reinforcing their capital ratios and liquidity positions by lowering their exposure in transactions such as loan commitments, and dividend pay-outs.

These results explain the lending behaviour of banks in the USA after the implementation of Basel III. Under Basel III, in addition to augmenting the level of minimum threshold of regulatory capital, banks are also required to hold minimum liquidity standards, which are the LCR and the NSF Ratio (NSFR).

DeYoung et al. (2018) and Cummings and Durrani (2016) investigated the effect of capital reserve requirements imposed by Basel Accords on Australian banks' practices regarding loan provisioning. The analysis found that banks increase the level of provisions in anticipation of future loan growth, by moving a portion of the surplus capital over capital requirements to fund future credit losses. The results also noted that banks allocate a percentage of their earnings to fund provision for credit losses. These results suggest that the increase of funds dedicated to provisions represents a reduction in liquidity that could have been allocated to funding loan offers.

Aiyar et al. (2016) analysed the interactions between UK's bank capital requirement regulation and banks' loan supply and found that tightening capital requirements has a reducing effect on the volume of credit offered by banks. This result indicates that banks in the UK would react to increases in bank capital requirements by lowering the volume of credit made available for their clients.

Gropp et al. (2019) studied the impact of capital regulations on banks' balance sheet, and their transmission to the real economy. The study found that banks reacted to increased regulatory requirements by reducing their credit volume to corporate and retail customers.

Imbierowicz et al. (2021) analysed the transmission in regulatory capital requirements and monetary policy, as well as their relationship with German banks' corporate lending growth and lending rates. The results suggested that increasing capital requirements led to an immediate reduction in total domestic and cross-border bank lending.

Abbas et al. (2020) found a positive relationship between bank CAR and bank liquidity for medium-sized banks and noted that a negative relationship between both variables is only confirmed for large commercial banks. These results indicate that the correlation between bank capital regulations and bank liquidity is dependent on bank size.

Additionally, De Jonghe et al. (2020) analysed the strategic lending decisions from banks facing a negative funding shock in Belgium. The analysis found that banks moved credit from within their loan portfolio in three key different ways: firstly, banks moved credits towards sectors where they have a high market share; secondly, they oriented their credit to specialised sectors; and thirdly, they shifted their credit towards sectors or firms rated as low risk. The study concluded that a standard deviation increase in sector market share, sector specialisation, or firm soundness lowers the transmission of the funding shock to credit supply by 22%, 8%, and 10%, respectively. This suggests that the reallocation effects have significant economic effects.

Gambacorta and Murcia (2020) summarised the results of a research project led by five Latin American central banks regarding the effectiveness of macroprudential policies and their interactions with monetary policy. The review found that macroprudential tools stabilised credit cycles. The effect of macroprudential tools on credit growth is higher for tools aimed at curbing the cycle, than for policies that focused on fostering economic resilience. Furthermore, Gropp et al. (2019) studied the impact of capital regulations on banks' balance sheet, and their transmission to the real economy. The study found that banks responded to higher regulatory capital reserve requirements by reducing their credit volume to corporate and retail customers.

The reshuffling of funds on banks' balance sheet is a topic studied by various researchers through various cross-country studies. These cross-country studies highlighted various aspects of this mechanism. Degryse et al. (2021) investigated the level of collateral set by banks on new loans, when they face higher capital requirements. The results found that after a financial shock, banks tend to require that borrowers provide higher levels of collateral to secure loans. This behaviour of banks is followed by the reallocation of bank liquidity to sectors that have greater asset tangibility.

These results explain the lending portfolio shifting response of banks when facing higher capital requirements. Comparable results were obtained by other researchers such as Klinac et al. (2019) who studied the activities of banks in response to new regulatory changes in the banking system in Europe. The results demonstrated that increasing the regulatory capital required from banks led to limiting bank credit to non-financial sectors.

In response to higher capital requirements, banks may finance their self-growth by increasing the volume of their share capital. Furthermore, De Jonghe et al. (2020) found that while macroprudential policy has the explicit goal for ensuring the resilience of the financial system, higher capital requirements lead to lower credit supply to corporations, as well as balance sheet adjustments.

Our study focused on the Canadian commercial and development banking, trading, and investment banking sector, as it is the main driver of Canadian banks' loan to the non-financial loan sector, which ultimately supports the real economy. We adapted pre-existing models applied in previous studies published by other scholars such as Benetton et al. (2021), Gambacorta and Shin (2018), Glancy and Kurtzman (2018), Juelsrud and Wold (2020), Brei and Moreno (2019), and Imbierowicz et al. (2021).

Firstly, the results of our studies determined that a 1% increase in Canadian regulatory bank capital requirement ratio led to a decrease in Corporate & Commercial Loans by 0.44% (Table 3.10). The results indicate that the decrease in Corporate & Commercial Loans following a 1% increase in Canadian regulatory bank capital requirement ratio is statistically significant (Table 3.10).

However, the results of our studies did not lead to statistically significant changes in Residential Mortgage Loans and Other Consumer/Retail Loans, following a 1% increase in Canadian regulatory bank capital requirement ratio. These results indicate that variations in Canadian regulatory bank capital requirement ratio had a direct downward effect on only the portion of Canadian banks' lending portfolio that accounts for Corporate & Commercial Loans. Our findings are in line with previous studies published by other scholars such as Aiyar et al. (2016), De Jonghe et al. (2020), and Imbierowicz et al. (2021), and Gropp et al. (2019).

In addition to confirming the results of the previous literature, our results contributed to the literature by determining that Retail Customer Loans and Residential Mortgages Loans are not directly impacted by changes in regulatory capital requirements. Only Corporate & Commercial Loans are negatively impacted by changes in Canadian regulatory bank capital requirements.

Secondly, we observed that the decrease in the portfolio of Canadian banks' loan to the non-financial sector, following increases in the Canadian regulatory bank capital requirements (1%), was estimated at 0.44% for Corporate & Commercial Loans. These decreases in credit represent a decrease of Corporate & Commercial Loans in billions of US dollars, given that the portion of the portfolio of Canadian banks' loan to the non-financial sector, which is equivalent to Corporate & Commercial Loans amounts for trillion of US dollars.

Thirdly, our results indicated that the impact of the increase (1%) in the Canadian regulatory bank capital requirements on Corporate & Commercial Loans (–0.44%) is not dependent on changes in bank control variables (Lagged (t–1) Return on Assets, Lagged (t–1) Excess Capital, Lagged (t–1) Ratio of Liquid Assets to Total Assets, Lagged (t–1) Bank Size, and Lagged (t–1) Ratio of Core Deposit), nor all macroeconomic control variables (GDP Gap, Business Climate, and Credit-to-GDP Gap). The results rather found that the impact of the increase in the Canadian regulatory bank capital requirements on Corporate & Commercial Loans is dependent on variations in economic policy.

Specifically, our studies found that a 1% increase in economic policy uncertainty led to a reduction in Corporate & Commercial Loans by 0.09%. This result indicates that favourable levels of business climate, as well as healthy bank level ratios; are not sufficient to reduce the negative impact of incremental changes in Canadian regulatory bank capital requirements on Corporate & Commercial Loans. Furthermore, economic policy uncertainty increases the severity of the effect of the variations of Canadian regulatory bank capital requirements on Corporate & Commercial Loans.

Fourthly, the results found that the change in Residential Mortgage Loans is not directly impacted by incremental changes in Canadian regulatory bank capital requirements. The change in Residential Mortgage Loans is rather dependent on the bank's Return on Asset over the previous year, and levels of Economic Policy uncertainty, following the increase of Canadian regulatory bank capital requirements. Specifically, the results found that increases of 1% in the bank's Return on Asset over the previous year, and Economic policy uncertainty, led to decreases in Residential

Mortgage Loans by 7.95% and 0.08% respectively, following the increase of Canadian regulatory bank capital requirements.

These results indicate that in times of economic policy uncertainty, Canadian banks with increased levels of Return on Asset over the previous year chose to reduce the level of their credit allocation for Residential Mortgage Loans, following an increase in Canadian regulatory bank capital requirements.

Fifthly, our results found that the level of credit portfolio allocation by Canadian banks towards other Consumer/Retail Loans is not directly impacted by variations of Canadian regulatory bank capital requirements. The level of credit portfolio allocation by Canadian banks to other Consumer/Retail Loans is rather controlled by macroeconomic variables such as GDP Gap, Business Climate, and Credit-to-GDP Gap.

Specifically, our results found that following 1% increases in GDP Gap, Credit-to-GDP Gap, and Canadian regulatory bank capital requirements, Canadian banks increased their level of credit portfolio allocation to Consumer/Retail Loans by 3.69% and 1.07%, respectively.

On the other hand, the results found that despite improvements in business climate by 1%, the level of credit portfolio allocated to Consumer/Retail Loans decreased by 4.36% following an increase in Canadian regulatory bank capital requirements (1%).

Overall, our results provide regulators and policymakers with empirical evidence highlighting the need to require different levels of capital requirements, targeting each of the following components of the portfolio of Canadian banks' loan to the non-financial sector: Corporate & Commercial Loans and Residential Mortgage Loans.

Furthermore, our studies offer regulators and policymakers with a set of key economic factors necessary to ensure increases in regulatory capital requirements on Corporate & Commercial Loans, and Residential Mortgage Loans do not lead to tighter liquidity to the non-financial sector, which could negatively impact recovery efforts from an economic downturn.

The remainder parts of this study are structured as follows: Section 4.2 provides details of research questions and hypotheses, Section 4.3 provides details on our sample data and variables, Section 4.4 presents empirical studies, Section 4.5 provides details of robustness checks, and Section 4.6 presents conclusions.

Figure 1: Summary of Research Question 3		
Gap in Literature	**Research Question**	**Hypothesis**
▪ Mixed results regarding the implications of changes in banks' regulatory capital requirements on Canadian banks' Gross Loan Portfolio. ▪ Limited literature regarding the impact of regulatory capital on Canadian banks' Gross Loan Portfolio.	What is the impact of banks' regulatory capital requirements on Canadian banks' Gross Loan Portfolio?	**H0**: Increase in banks' regulatory capital requirements **leads to a decrease** in the components of Canadian banks' Gross Loan Portfolio. **H1**: Increase in banks' regulatory capital requirements **leads to an increase** in the components of Canadian banks' Gross Loan Portfolio. **H2**: Increase in banks' regulatory capital requirements **leads to no impact** on the components of Canadian banks' Gross Loan Portfolio.

Fig. 4.1 Summary of research question 3

4.2 Research Questions and Hypotheses

The literature review presented in the previous section revealed the existence of mixed results regarding the implications of changes in banks' regulatory capital requirements on banks' lending behaviour.

Furthermore, the literature review also revealed that there were no studies regarding the impact of regulatory capital requirements on the lending portfolio of Canadian banks. The conclusions of the literature review led to the following research question:

- **Research Question 3:** *What is the impact of banks' regulatory capital requirements on Canadian banks' Gross Loan Portfolio?*

Figure 4.1 presents a summary of the third research question and relevant hypothesis.

4.3 Data and Variables

This study uses the annual financial statistics of Canadian financial institutions from 2012 to 2021, from Fitch Connect database.[1] The aggregate

[1] Fitch Solutions, Canadian Bank Financials Data, from 2012 to 2021. Available from Fitch Solutions. July 2022.

total asset value of the entire Canadian banking industry over the period of 2012 to 2021 is 5.2 trillion USD. Universal Commercial Banks, Wholesale Commercial Banks, Development Banks, Investment and Trading Banks hold 4.8 trillion USD in aggregate total assets, over the same period. Our sample covers Universal Commercial Banks, Wholesale Commercial Banks, Development Banks, and Investment and Trading Banks, representing 120 Canadian banks, and accounting for 92% of the Canadian banking sector, in terms of aggregate total assets over the period of 2012 to 2021. Our sample also covers GDP Gap statistics from the Bank of Canada,[2] Credit-to-GDP Gap statistics from the BIS,[3] Business Climate outlook statistics[4] from the Bank of Canada, and the Canada News-Based Policy Uncertainty Index from the Economic Policy Uncertainty Research Group,[5] from 2012 and 2021.

Our study focuses on the Canadian commercial, development, investment, and trading banking sector, given that it is the main vehicle of lending to the non-financial sector, which supports the real economy. Contrarily to the financial economy which covers transactions of money and financial assets, the real economy is more connected to economic growth and encompasses the production and distribution of goods and services. Furthermore, corporate loans to the non-financial sector tend to have shorter debt maturities, aligning more with changes in regulatory capital requirements. The data used encompassed the portfolio decomposition of the Gross Loans observations analysed in the first model and presented in Chapter 2 of this book.

The study investigated the impact of changes in regulatory capital requirements on the components of the portfolio of loan offered by Canadian banks to the non-financial sector. The portfolio of loan offered by Canadian banks to the non-financial sector encompasses the following components: Corporate & Commercial Loans (26% of Gross Loan), Other Mortgage Loans (6% of Gross Loan), Residential Mortgage Loans (44% of Gross Loan), Other Loans and Loan-related balances (4% of Gross Loan),

[2] Bank of Canada, Product Market: Definitions, Graphs and Data. Estimates of the Output Gap. Available from https://www.bankofcanada.ca/?p=39818. July 2022.

[3] The Bank for International Settlements, Credit-to-GDP Trend (HP Filter). Available from https://stats.bis.org/statx/srs/table/f2.1?p=20174&c=. July 2022.

[4] Bank of Canada, Business Outlook Survey Data. Available from https://www.bankofcanada.ca/publications/bos/business-outlook-survey-data/. July 2022.

[5] Economic Policy Uncertainty Research Group, News-Based Policy Uncertainty Index. Available from Economic Policy Uncertainty Index. July 2022.

and Other Consumer/Retail Loans (20% of Gross Loan). Our studies will focus on the three largest components of the portfolio of loan offered by Canadian banks to the non-financial sector: Corporate & Commercial Loans (26% of Gross Loan), Residential Mortgage Loans (44% of Gross Loan), and Other Consumer/Retail Loans (20% of Gross Loan).

We measured the annual variation of Corporate & Commercial Loans by calculating the year over year change in Corporate & Commercial Loans. Similar approach was applied to the annual variation of Residential Mortgage Loans and Other Consumer/Retail Loans.

The introduction of Basel III in 2010 required banks to maintain a minimum CAR of 8%, which is determined considering Tier 1 capital and Tier 2 capital only, eliminating Tier 3 capital from the CAR calculation.[6]

The OSFI[7] defines Total regulatory capital as Tier 1 regulatory capital plus Tier 2 capital. Tier 1 regulatory capital is the aggregation of Common Equity Tier 1 (CET1) capital and Additional Tier 1 capital.

OSFI[8] defines Tier 2 capital (prior to regulatory adjustments) as the sum of the following items: Instruments issued by the financial institution that meet the criteria for inclusion in Tier 2 capital (and are not included in Tier 1 capital); surplus (share premium) emanating from the issue of instruments included in Tier 2 capital; instruments issued by consolidated subsidiaries of the financial institution and held by third parties that meet the criteria for inclusion in Tier 2 capital (and are not included in Tier 1 capital); and certain loan loss allowances that meet the criteria for inclusion in Tier 2 capital.

OSFI[9] defines total regulatory capital requirements (Total Reg Cap Ratio) as the sum of risk-based capital ratios, conservation buffer, and a countercyclical buffer (where applicable). Risk-based capital ratios are calculated by dividing total capital (Total Reg Cap) by the sum of credit,

[6] Basel Committee on Banking Supervision, History of the Basel Committee (Basel III: Responding to the 2007-09 Financial Crisis). Available from https://www.bis.org/bcbs/history.htm. April 2022.

[7] Office of the Superintendent of Financial Institutions, Requirements for Inclusion in Regulatory Capital. Available from https://www.osfi-bsif.gc.ca/en/guidance/guidance-library/capital-adequacy-requirements-car-2024-chapter-2-definition-capital. July 2022.

[8] Office of the Superintendent of Financial Institutions, Tier 2 Capital. Available from https://www.osfi-bsif.gc.ca/en/guidance/guidance-library/capital-adequacy-requirements-car-2024-chapter-2-definition-capital. July 2022.

[9] Office of the Superintendent of Financial Institutions, Calculation of OSFI Minimum Capital Requirements. Available from https://www.osfi-bsif.gc.ca/Eng/fi-if/rg-ro/gdn-ort/gl-ld/Pages/CAR22_chpt1.aspx. July 2022.

operational, and market RWAs. OSFI requires Canadian banks to maintain a minimum capital requirement ratio, in addition to a conservation buffer (where applicable), a countercyclical buffer (where applicable), and Basel III leverage ratio.

Canadian banks are regulated by the OSFI and are required to abide by regulatory capital requirements set by OSFI. Our study used the annual variation in (Total regulatory capital ratios + Basel III leverage ratios) disclosed to OSFI by Canadian banks, as part of their annual financial disclosure.

$$\Delta \textit{ in Total Reg Cap Ratio} = \Delta \textit{ in} \frac{\text{Total Reg Cap}}{\text{RWA}} + \Delta \textit{ in Basel III Leverage Ratio}$$

Our study used lagged values of Return on Assets, Ratio of Liquid Assets to Total Assets, Bank Size, Ratio of Core Deposits, and Excess Capital Ratio to account for bank effects.

The lagged values of Return on Assets and Ratio of Liquid Assets to Total Assets were calculated using the values of Return on Assets and Ratio of Liquid Assets to Total Assets, disclosed by the Canadian bank in the previous year (t–1).

The lagged value of Ratio of Core Deposits was obtained by using the lagged Ratio of Total Customer Deposits to Total Assets.

The lagged value of Bank Size is the lagged value of the logarithm of Total Assets.

Basel III[10] requires banks to maintain additional countercyclical capital buffers for times of economic downturn. The percentage of countercyclical capital buffers could range between 0 and 2.5%. Under Basel III, the local banking supervision regulator (OSFI for Canadian banks) could opt for the imposition of the highest required countercyclical capital buffer of 2.5%, leading to a minimum CAR of 10.5%. We calculated the lagged excess capital ratio (Lagged Ex Cap Ratio) by subtracting the minimum CAR of 10.5% under Basel III (Min Basel III Cap Ratio of 10.5%) from the Total regulatory capital ratio of the bank and lagging the result.

$$\text{Lagged }(t-1)\text{ Ex Cap Ratio} = \text{Lagged }(t-1)\begin{bmatrix}\text{Total Reg Cap Ratio}\\ -\text{Min Basel III Cap Ratio of } 10.5\%\end{bmatrix}$$

[10] Basel Committee on Banking Supervision, The Capital Buffers in Basel III – Executive Summary. Available from https://www.bis.org/bcbs/history.htm. July 2022.

Variables measuring Economic Policy uncertainty, GDP Gap, Business Climate, and Credit-to-GDP Gap were introduced to control for macroeconomic effects.

Economic Policy uncertainty is measured using the yearly average of Canada News-Based Policy Uncertainty Index, published by the Economic Policy Uncertainty Research Group.[11]

GDP Gap is measured by yearly average of output gap, which is the deviation of actual GDP from potential output, published by the Bank of Canada.[12]

Credit-to-GDP Gap is measured by the delta between credit-to-GDP ratio and its long-term trend, published by the BIS.[13]

Business Climate is measured by the yearly BOS indicator, published by the Bank of Canada.[14]

A fixed effect model (Panel Data Regression) enables the control for all time-invariant differences between observed entities. This ensures that the coefficients of the time effect model are not biased due to the non-inclusion or omission of time-invariant characteristics of the entity.

In the case of our research, the time-invariant characteristics could be the bank's corporate culture, bank's internal policy, and bank's management strategy.

However, time-invariant characteristics such as bank's corporate culture, bank's internal policy, and bank's management strategy could also be classified as time-variant characteristics. Bank's corporate culture, bank's internal policy, and bank's management strategy could be modified multiple times during a year.

In the empirical study, we included bank control variables which are the results of the bank's corporate culture, bank's internal policy, and bank's management strategy.

In the empirical study of the effect of changes in regulatory capital requirements on the components of the portfolio of loan offered by Canadian banks to the non-financial sector, the bank control variables

[11] Economic Policy Uncertainty Research Group, News-Based Policy Uncertainty Index. Available from Economic Policy Uncertainty Index. July 2022.

[12] Bank of Canada, Product Market: Definitions, Graphs and Data. Estimates of the Output Gap. Available from https://www.bankofcanada.ca/?p=39818. July 2022.

[13] The Bank for International Settlements, Credit-to-GDP Trend (HP Filter). Available from https://stats.bis.org/statx/srs/table/f2.1?p=20174&c=. July 2022.

[14] Bank of Canada, Business Outlook Survey Data. Available from https://www.bankofcanada.ca/publications/bos/business-outlook-survey-data/. July 2022.

account for lagged values of Excess capital, Return on Assets, Ratio of Liquid Assets to Total Assets, Bank Size, and Ratio of Core Deposits.

The values of the bank control variables incorporate the effect of banks' internal characteristics. Therefore, the incorporation of the bank control variables in the multiple regression controls for effects of banks' internal characteristics. Furthermore, given that the differences between the banks (entities) are correlated with predictors (bank control variables), a random effect model (Panel Model Regression) does not emerge as an option.

Komath et al. (2023) studied the impact of corporate governance and related controversies on the market value of banks. The results of their study found that there is a statistically significant relationship between the corporate governance controversies scores and the market value of banks.

Barth and Mansouri (2021) studied the role of corporate culture in banking. The authors found that corporate culture is a softer aspect of governance necessary to enhance banking stability. Specifically, they found that banks with a more pronounced competition-oriented culture have stronger bonus-focused compensation schemes. Banks with a strong focus on growth demonstrated higher stock returns, and finally, banks with a focus on stability had lower bankruptcy risk.

Table 4.1 presents a summarised description of variables.

The statistics on Canadian banks' loan portfolio showed some spurious outliers. Hence, we transformed the statistics through winsorisation to limit the effect of extreme values or spurious outliers.

Table 4.2 presents descriptive statistics following winsorisation.

Table 4.2 (Descriptive Statistics) shows that the average annual variation of Corporate & Commercial Loans, Residential Mortgage Loans, and Other Consumer/Retail Loans is respectively 3.20%, 6.70%, and –1.03%, while the yearly change in regulatory capital requirements is 2.08% on average.

Table 4.3 presents the annual average change in regulatory capital requirements and the annual average change in Canadian banks' gross loan portfolio to the non-financial sector, following winsorisation.

The observations of the annual average change in regulatory capital requirements and the annual average change in Canadian banks' gross loan portfolio to the non-financial sector, following winsorisation (Table 4.3), indicate that increases in regulatory capital requirements led to a decrease in all of the components of Canadian banks' gross loan portfolio, during the years 2014 and 2015.

However, further analysis is necessary to ascertain the true impact of regulatory capital requirements on each of the components of Canadian banks' gross loan portfolio. The subsequent pages will provide a detailed empirical study.

Table 4.1 Description of variables

	Definition	*Data Source*
Independent Variables		
Annual Δ Corporate & Commercial Loans (Corporate & Commercial Loans account for 26% of Canadian Banks' Gross Loans to the non-financial sector)	Annual Δ in Canadian Banks' Corporate & Commercial Loans to the non-financial sector. Canadian Banks' Corporate & Commercial Loans to the non-financial sector were obtained from Fitch Connect Database.	Fitch Connect Database
Annual Δ Residential Mortgage Loans (Residential Mortgage Loans account for 44% of Canadian Banks' Gross Loans to the non-financial sector)	Annual Δ in Canadian Banks' Residential Mortgage Loans to the non-financial sector. Canadian Banks' Residential Mortgage Loans to the non-financial sector were obtained from Fitch Connect Database.	Fitch Connect Database
Annual Δ Other Consumer/ Retail Loans (Other Consumer/Retail Loans account for 20% of Canadian Banks' Gross Loans to the non-financial sector)	Annual Δ in Canadian Banks' Other Consumer/Retail Loans to the non-financial sector. Canadian Banks' Other Consumer/Retail Loans to the non-financial sector were obtained from Fitch Connect Database.	Fitch Connect Database
Independent Variable		
Annual Δ Canadian Bank Capital Requirements	Annual variation in (Total regulatory capital ratios + Basel III leverage ratios) disclosed to OSFI by Canadian banks, as part of their annual financial disclosure.	Fitch Connect Database
Bank Effects Control Variables		
Lagged (t–1) Excess capital	Lagged excess capital ratio is calculated by subtracting the minimum CAR of 10.5% under Basel III from the Total regulatory capital ratio of the bank (Total Reg Cap Ratio) and taking the lagging the result. We adopted a conservative approach for the calculation of Lagged (t–1) Excess capital by utilising the most stringent minimum capital requirement.	Fitch Connect Database
Lagged (t–1) Return on Assets	Lagged Return on Assets	Fitch Connect Database
Lagged (t–1) Ratio of Liquid Assets to Total Assets	Lagged Ratio of Liquid Assets to Total Assets	Fitch Connect Database
Lagged (t–1) Bank Size	Lagged Logarithm of Total Assets	Fitch Connect Database

Table 4.1 (continued)

	Definition	*Data Source*
Lagged (t–1) Ratio of Core Deposit	Lagged Ratio of Total Core Deposits (Total Customer Deposits) to Total Assets	Fitch Connect Database
Macroeconomic Control Variable		
Economic Policy	Yearly Average of Canada News-Based Policy Uncertainty Index	Economic Policy Uncertainty Research Group
GDP Gap	Deviation of actual GDP from potential output (Yearly Average of output gap)	Bank of Canada
Business Climate	Canadian BOS Indicator (Yearly Average of BOS Indicator)	Bank of Canada
Credit-to-GDP Gap	Deviation of credit to GDP from its long-term trend (BIS Statistics)	Bank for International Settlements (BIS)

4.4 Results

We analysed the effect of changes in regulatory capital requirements on the components of the portfolio of loan offered by Canadian banks to the non-financial sector. The portfolio of loan offered by Canadian banks to the non-financial sector encompasses the following components: Corporate & Commercial Loans (26% of Gross Loan), Other Mortgage Loans (6% of Gross Loan), Residential Mortgage Loans (44% of Gross Loan), Other Loans and Loan-related balances (4% of Gross Loan), and Other Consumer/Retail Loans (20% of Gross Loan). Our studies will focus on the three largest components of the portfolio of loan offered by Canadian banks to the non-financial sector: Corporate & Commercial Loans (26% of Gross Loan), Residential Mortgage Loans (44% of Gross Loan), and Other Consumer/Retail Loans (20% of Gross Loan). The data used encompassed the portfolio decomposition of the Gross Loans observations analysed in the first model, presented Chapter 2 of this book.

Our empirical studies adapted pre-existing models, previously applied by other researchers such as Aiyar et al. (2016), De Jonghe et al. (2020), and Imbierowicz et al. (2021), for the study of changes of capital requirements and corporate lending in other jurisdictions, other than Canada.

The adaptation of pre-existing models ensures our studies follow a scientific rigour and enables the comparison of our results with those of previous studies. Our model is also the result of the application of econometric methods and principles from Gourieroux and Jasiak (2018), Campbell et al. (1996), as well as research methods' recommendations from Chevalier et al. (2019).

Additionally, our model is also the result of the application of knowledge acquired through the literature review, as well as professional and managerial experiences. The validity and goodness-of-fit of our model is demonstrated through the model statistics, regression assumption tests and robustness tests presented in subsequent sections.

Table 4.2 Descriptive statistics

	Mean	*Standard Deviation*
Dependent Variables		
Annual Δ Corporate & Commercial Loans	3.20	25.96
Annual Δ Residential Mortgage Loans	6.70	24.24
Annual Δ Other Consumer/Retail Loans	–1.03	29.92
Independent Variable		
Annual Δ Canadian Bank Capital Requirements	2.08	11.22
Bank Control Variables		
Lagged (t–1) Return on Assets	0.66	0.60
Lagged (t–1) Excess Capital	20.20	12.18
Lagged (t–1) Ratio of Liquid Assets to Total Assets	16.17	15.21
Lagged (t–1) Bank Size	3.71	1.00
Lagged (t–1) Ratio of Core Deposit	67.24	22.93
Macroeconomic Control Variable		
Economic Policy	264.47	92.33
GDP Gap	–1.89	2.05
Business Climate	–0.09	1.79
Credit-to-GDP Gap	205.47	14.90
Other Details		
Observations – Annual Δ Corporate & Commercial Loans 153		
Observations – Annual Δ Residential Mortgage Loans 191		
Observations – Annual Δ Other Consumer/Retail Loans 212		

Note: Shown are the descriptive statistics using financial statistics of Canadian financial institutions and macroeconomic data, from 2012 to 2021, for variables described in Table 4.1.

Adapting pre-existing models used by Aiyar et al. (2016), De Jonghe et al. (2020), and Imbierowicz et al. (2021), we analysed the effect of changes in regulatory capital requirements on the components of the portfolio of loan offered by Canadian banks to the non-financial sector, applying the following multiple regression model:

$$\Delta \mathbf{Y}_{\mathbf{a,t}} = \propto_0 + \sum_{t=1}^{10} \alpha_{1,t} \Delta \mathbf{Cap}_{\mathbf{a,t}} + \beta \mathbf{X}_{\mathbf{a,t-1}} + f_a + \varepsilon_{\mathbf{a,t}} \qquad \text{(Model 3)}$$

where $\Delta \mathbf{Y}_{\mathbf{a,t}}$ is the variation (year over year change) in the components of Canadian bank 'a' gross lending portfolio following changes in regulatory capital requirements in year 't'.

The portfolio of loan offered by Canadian banks to the non-financial sector encompasses the following three main components: Corporate & Commercial Loans (26% of Gross Loan), Residential Mortgage Loans (44% of Gross Loan), and Other Consumer/Retail Loans (20% of Gross Loan).

The annual variation of Corporate & Commercial Loans is obtained by calculating the year over year change in Corporate & Commercial Loans. Similar approach was applied to the annual variation of Residential Mortgage Loans, and Other Consumer/Retail Loans.

Table 4.3 Annual Average of Changes in Regulatory Capital Requirements and Canadian Banks' Gross Loan Portfolio

Year	*Mean of Annual Δ Canadian Bank Capital Requirements*	*Mean of Annual Δ Bank Commercial Loan*	*Mean of Annual Δ Bank Residential Loan*	*Mean of Annual Δ Bank Consumer/ Retail Loan*
2012	–	–	–	–
2013	12.51	9.02	7.83	–0.44
2014	**11.40**	**–3.74**	**–0.69**	**–8.13**
2015	**2.89**	**–7.86**	**–1.90**	**–7.86**
2016	3.2	10.33	16.09	–1.71
2017	1.70	8.32	14.50	–0.065
2018	–0.69	1.87	2.15	–2.37
2019	3.62	1.91	5.79	10.33
2020	2.22	–5.61	4.05	0.16
2021	2.72	19.02	15.23	1.64

Note: Shown are the average changes in regulatory capital requirements and the average changes in Canadian banks' gross loan portfolio to the non-financial sector, annually, following winsorisation.

$\Delta \mathbf{Cap}_{a,t}$ is the change in regulatory bank capital requirement ratio for bank 'a', during year 't'. $\Delta \mathbf{Cap}_{a,t}$ is calculated using the annual variation in (Total regulatory capital ratios + Basel III leverage ratios) disclosed to OSFI by Canadian banks, as part of their annual financial disclosure.

$$\Delta \text{ in Total Reg Cap Ratio} = \Delta \text{ in} \frac{\text{Total Reg Cap}}{\text{RWA}} + \Delta \text{ in Basel III Leverage Ratio}$$

We introduced a vector of lagged bank-specific variables to control for bank effects. $\mathbf{X}_{a,t-1}$ represents a vector of lagged bank-specific control variables, capturing the Return on Assets, Excess Capital, Ratio of Liquid Assets to Total Assets, Bank Size, and Ratio of core Deposits to Total Assets.

The lagged values of Return on Assets and Ratio of Liquid Assets to Total Assets were calculated using the values of Return on Assets and Ratio of Liquid Assets to Total Assets, disclosed by the Canadian bank in the previous year (t–1).

The lagged value of Excess Capital Ratio (Lagged (t–1) Ex Cap Ratio) was calculated by subtracting the minimum CAR of 10.5% under Basel III (Min Basel III Cap Ratio of 10.5%) from the Total regulatory capital ratio of the bank and lagging the value of the result (Lagged (t–1) Total Reg Cap Ratio).

The lagged value of Ratio of Core Deposits was obtained by using the lagged Ratio of Total Customer Deposits to Total Assets.

The lagged value of Bank Size is the lagged value of the logarithm of Total Assets.

f_a is the vector of macroeconomic control variables introduced to control for macroeconomic effects. Variables measuring Economic Policy uncertainty, GDP Gap, Business Climate, and Credit-to-GDP Gap were introduced to control for macroeconomic effects.

Table 4.4 presents the results of the Multivariate Analysis of Variance (MANOVA), which determines whether the independent variables or their combination have an effect on the dependent variables.

The F probability for each of the four levels of test (Wilks' lambda, Pillai's trace, Lawley-Hotelling trace, Roy's largest root) of the MANOVA is statistically significant (F Prob < 0.05). The test of the overall MANOVA model indicates that the independent variables or their combination have an effect on the dependent variables, described in the multiple regression model presented above (Model 3).

Table 4.5 presents the results of the multiple regression analysing the effect of changes in regulatory capital requirements on the three largest

Table 4.4 Multivariate analysis of variance

Source	*Statistic*	*df*	*F (df1*	*df2)*	*F*	*= F Prob>F*
Model W (W= Wilks' lambda)	0.6463	10	30.0	311.8	1.67	0.0180 a
Model P (P= Pillai's trace)	0.4000		30.0	324.0	1.66	0.0184 a
Model L (L = Lawley-Hotelling trace)	0.4783		30.0	314.0	1.67	0.0177 a
Model R (R= Roy's largest root)	0.2709		10.0	108.0	2.93	0.0028 u
Residual						108
Total						118

e = exact, a = approximate, u = upper bound on F

components of the portfolio of loan (Corporate & Commercial Loans, Residential Mortgage Loans, and Other Consumer/Retail Loans) offered by Canadian banks to the non-financial sector.

We tested regression assumptions supporting our multiple regression model. Table 4.6 presents the results of the Shapiro–Wilk W test for normal data.

The *p* value of the Shapiro–Wilk W test (*p* value of 0.00) confirmed that r is not normally distributed. Therefore, we conducted a non-parametric test (Kruskal–Wallis) to control for non-normality. Table 4.7 presents the results of the Kruskal–Wallis equality-of-populations rank test.

The *p* value of the Kruskal–Wallis equality-of-populations rank test is over 0.05 ($p > 0.05$). Therefore, the null hypothesis is accepted, and we can confirm that the annual variation of Corporate & Commercial Loans, Residential Mortgage Loans, and Other Consumer/Retail Loans, and the yearly change in total bank capital requirement ratios follow the same statistical distribution.

Table 4.8 presents the results of test of autocorrelation (Breusch–Godfrey LM test).

The *p* value of the Breusch–Godfrey LM test is over 0.05 ($p > 0.05$). Therefore, the null hypothesis is accepted, and we can confirm that there is no serial correlation (no autocorrelation).

Table 4.9 presents the results of the test of multicollinearity.

We tested for multicollinearity using the VIF, which measures the value of multicollinearity amongst regression variables. The test found a VIF value lower to 10 (<10), indicating that there is no multicollinearity.

Table 4.10 presents the results of the test of homoscedasticity of residuals (Breusch–Pagan/Cook–Weisberg test for heteroscedasticity).

Table 4.5 Impact of changes in bank regulatory capital requirements on Canadian banks' loan portfolio (multiple regression)

	Annual Δ Corp. & Commercial Loans	*Annual Δ Residential Mortgage Loans*	*Annual Δ Other Consumer/ Retail Loans*
Independent Variables			
Annual Δ Canadian Bank Capital Requirements	**−0.44** **(0.02)****	**−0.27** **(0.08)***	0.09 (0.62)
Bank Control Variables			
Lagged (t–1) Return on Assets	1.45 (0.77)	**−7.95** **(0.03)****	4.87 (0.29)
Lagged (t–1) Excess Capital	−0.07 (0.78)	0.17 (0.40)	−0.03 (0.90)
Lagged (t–1) Ratio of Liquid Assets to Total Assets	0.13 (0.43)	0.05 (0.67)	0.03 (0.83)
Lagged (t–1) Bank Size	2.77 (0.27)	−2.20 (0.35)	1.30 (0.66)
Lagged (t–1) Ratio of Core Deposit	**0.20** **(0.10)***	−0.03 (0.73)	0.15 (0.21)
Macro. Control Variables			
Economic Policy	**−0.09** **(0.05)***	**−0.08** **(0.05)****	−0.05 (0.37)
GDP Gap	−0.87 (0.54)	−1.01 (0.43)	**3.69** **(0.02)****
Business Climate	1.40 (0.50)	−0.53 (0.77)	**−4.36** **(0.07)***
Credit-to-GDP Gap	0.34 (0.47)	0.32 (0.44)	**1.07** **(0.05)****
Other Details			
R^2	0.1748	0.1220	0.0425
Number of banks	120	120	120
Observations	153	191	212

Note: Shown are the results of the multiple regression analysis using the multiple regression model presented above. The statistical significance of results is indicated by *10% level, **5% level and ***1% level using standard errors. *p* values are presented in parentheses after coefficient estimates.

Table 4.6 Shapiro–Wilk W test for normal data

Variable	*Obs*	*W*	*V*	*Z*	*Prob>z*
R	153	0.94874	6.067	4.091	0.00002

The *p* value of the Cameron & Trivedi's decomposition of IM test and White's test for heteroscedasticity is 0.00. Therefore, the null hypothesis is rejected, and we can confirm that the variance of residuals is not homogenous (heteroscedasticity). The presence of heteroscedasticity could be due subpopulation differences, model misspecifications, or measurement errors. Therefore, we re-estimated the initial model, introducing robust standard errors to correct the effects of heteroscedasticity.

Table 4.11 presents the results of the multiple regression analysing the effect of changes in regulatory capital requirements on the components of the portfolio of loan offered by Canadian banks to the non-financial sector, with the introduction of robust standard errors.

The *p* values related to the robust standard errors (Table 4.11) are different to the *p* values related to the standard errors obtained in the initial multiple regression model estimation (Table 4.5). The issue of heteroscedasticity has been resolved, with the introduction of robust standard errors.

Firstly, our results found that a 1% increase in Canadian regulatory bank capital requirement ratio led to a decrease in Corporate & Commercial Loans by 0.44%. The results supporting the decrease in Corporate & Commercial Loans, following a 1% increase in Canadian regulatory bank capital requirement ratio are statistically significant (Table 4.11).

Table 4.7 Non-parametric test to control for non-normality (Kruskal–Wallis equality-of-populations rank test)

Dependent Variable	*Chi2*	*Prob*
Annual Δ Corp. & Commercial Loans	Chi2 (140) = 135.43	0.59
	Chi2 (140) with ties = 135.46	0.59
Annual Δ Resid. Mortgage Loans	Chi2 (165) = 161.37	0.56
	Chi2 (165) with ties = 161.43	0.56
Annual Δ Other Cons./Retail	Chi2 (186) = 183.47	0.53
	Chi2 (186) with ties = 183.57	0.53

Note: Kruskal–Wallis equality-of-populations rank test for Annual Δ Corp. & Commercial Loans, Annual Δ Resid. Mortgage Loans, and Annual Δ Other Cons./Retail Loans.

Table 4.8 Test of autocorrelation (Breusch–Godfrey LM test)

Dependent Variable	*lags(p)*	*chi2*	*df*	*Prob > chi2*
Annual Δ Corp. & Commercial Loans	1	1.66	1	0.19
Annual Δ Resid. Mortgage Loans	1	2.94	1	0.08
Annual Δ Other Cons./Retail	1	2.369	1	0.12

On the other hand, the results did not lead to statistically significant changes in Residential Mortgage Loans and Other Consumer/Retail Loans, following a 1% increase in Canadian regulatory bank capital requirement ratio (Table 4.11).

The results suggest that changes in Canadian regulatory bank capital requirement ratio had a direct downward impact on only the portion of Canadian lending portfolio that accounts for Corporate & Commercial Loans.

The findings are in line with previous studies, which found that banks responded to higher regulatory requirements by reducing their credit volume to the non-financial sector (Aiyar et al. 2016, De Jonghe et al. 2020, and Imbierowicz et al. 2021), and specifically by reducing their credit volume to corporate and retail customers (Gropp et al. 2019).

Table 4.9 Test of multicollinearity (VIF)

Dependent Variables	*Mean VIF*
Annual Δ Corp. & Commercial Loans	2.77
Annual Δ Resid. Mortgage Loans	2.80
Annual Δ Other Cons./Retail	2.83

Table 4.10 Test of homoscedasticity of residuals (Cameron & Trivedi's decomposition of IM test & White's test)

	Cameron & Trivedi's Decomposition of IM Test	*chi2*	*df*	*p*
Annual Δ Corp. & Commercial Loans	Heteroscedasticity	132.64	69	0.0000
	White's Test			
	H0: Homoscedasticity	chi2(58) = 88.98		
	Ha: Unrestricted heteroscedasticity	Prob > chi2 = 0.0055		
Annual Δ Resid. Mortgage Loans	Heteroscedasticity	156.24	69	0.0000
	White's Test			
	H0: Homoscedasticity	chi2(59) = 110.18		
	Ha: Unrestricted heteroscedasticity	Prob > chi2 = 0.0001		
Annual Δ Other Cons./Retail	Heteroscedasticity	149.37	70	0.0000
	White's Test			
	H0: Homoscedasticity	chi2 (59) = 110.18		
	Ha: Unrestricted heteroscedasticity	Prob > chi2 = 0.0001		

Table 4.11 Impact of changes in bank regulatory capital requirements on Canadian banks' loan portfolio, with the introduction of robust standard errors

	Annual Δ Corp. & Commercial Loans	*Annual Δ Residential Mortgage Loans*	*Annual Δ Other Consumer/Retail Loans*
Independent Variables			
Annual Δ Canadian Bank Capital Requirements	**−0.44** **(0.10)***	−0.27 (0.23)	0.09 (0.64)
Bank Control Variables			
Lagged (t−1) Return on Assets	1.45 (0.76)	**−7.95** **(0.09)***	4.87 (0.35)
Lagged (t−1) Excess Capital	−0.07 (0.82)	0.17 (0.50)	−0.03 (0.90)
Lagged (t−1) Ratio of Liquid Assets to Total Assets	0.13 (0.33)	0.05 (0.76)	0.03 (0.87)
Lagged (t−1) Bank Size	2.77 (0.24)	−2.20 (0.36)	1.30 (0.64)
Lagged (t−1) Ratio of Core Deposit	0.20 (0.18)	−0.03 (0.79)	0.15 (0.24)
Macro. Control Variables			
Economic Policy	**−0.09** **(0.07)***	**−0.08** **(0.04)****	−0.05 (0.35)
GDP Gap	−0.87 (0.52)	−1.01 (0.33)	**3.69** **(0.02)****
Business Climate	1.40 (0.52)	−0.53 (0.75)	**−4.36** **(0.06)***
Credit-to-GDP Gap	0.34 (0.47)	0.32 (0.39)	**1.07** **(0.05)****
Other Details			
R^2	0.1748	0.1220	0.6126
Number of banks	120	120	120
Observations	153	191	212

Note: Shown are the results of the multiple regression analysis using the multiple regression model presented above and introducing robust standard errors. The statistical significance of results is indicated by *10% level, **5% level and *** 1% level using robust standard errors. *p* values are presented in parentheses after coefficient estimates.

In addition to confirming the results of the previous literature, our results found that Residential Mortgage Loans and Other Consumer/Retail Loans are not directly impacted by changes in regulatory capital requirements. Only Corporate & Commercial Loans are directly and negatively impacted by increases in Canadian regulatory bank capital requirements.

The decreases in the portfolio of Canadian banks' loan to the non-financial sector, following increases in the Canadian regulatory bank capital requirements (1%) accounted for 0.44% for Corporate & Commercial Loans. These decreases in credit represent a reduction of Corporate & Commercial Loans in billions of US dollars, given that the portion of the portfolio of Canadian banks' loan to the non-financial sector, that account for Corporate & Commercial Loans amounts for trillions of US dollars.

Secondly, the results indicate that the impact of the increase (1%) in the Canadian regulatory bank capital requirements on Corporate & Commercial Loans (–0.44%) is not dependent on changes in bank control variables (Lagged (t–1) Return on Assets, Lagged (t–1) Excess Capital, Lagged (t–1) Ratio of Liquid Assets to Total Assets, Lagged (t–1) Bank Size, and Lagged (t–1) Ratio of Core Deposit), and macroeconomic control variables, except Economic Policy uncertainty (GDP Gap, Business Climate, and Credit-to-GDP Gap).

However, the results indicate that the impact of the increase in the Canadian regulatory bank capital requirements on Corporate & Commercial Loans is dependent on changes in economic policy. A 1% increase in economic policy uncertainty led to a decrease in Corporate & Commercial Loans by 0.09%.

This result suggests that favourable business climate as well as healthy bank level ratios are not sufficient to attenuate the negative impact of increases in the Canadian regulatory bank capital requirements on Corporate & Commercial Loans. Furthermore, economic policy uncertainty increases the severity of the impact of the change of Canadian regulatory bank capital requirements on Corporate & Commercial Loans.

Times of economic policy uncertainty are partly driven by unfavourable economic policies and characterised by negative economic indicators such as high inflation, high interest rates, and high unemployment. Therefore, regulators and policymakers should:

- Design and implement *forecasting methodologies* that enable the determination of the *optimal level of Canadian regulatory bank capital requirements on Corporate & Commercial Loans*. The imposition of Canadian regulatory bank capital requirements on Corporate & Commercial Loans beyond its optimal level can lead to sharp decreases in liquidity and credit allocation towards the non-financial Corporate & Commercial sector.

- *Only increase regulatory capital* requirements on *Corporate & Commercial Loans* prior to or post-economic downturns when a *combination of the following four favourable economic policy* factors is fulfilled:
  (i) Full employment,
  (ii) Economic expansion and growth,
  (iii) Price stability through the application of monetary policy tools, and
  (iv) Expansionary fiscal policy.
  This will ensure appropriate mitigation of liquidity shocks during times of economic downturn, ensuring economic recovery efforts are not negatively impacted by the effects of stricter regulatory capital requirements.

Thirdly, the results found that the change in Residential Mortgage Loans is not directly impacted by increases in Canadian regulatory bank capital requirements. The change in Residential Mortgage Loans is rather dependent on the bank's Return on Asset over the previous year, and the level of economic policy uncertainty, following increases in Canadian regulatory bank capital requirements.

Specifically, the results indicate that increases of 1% in the bank's Return on Asset over the previous year, and increases by 1% in economic policy uncertainty, led to decreases in Residential Mortgage Loans by 7.95% and 0.08% respectively, following a 1% increase in Canadian regulatory bank capital requirements.

These results suggest that in times of increasing economic policy uncertainty, Canadian banks with increasing return on asset over the previous year opted to decrease the level of their credit allocation towards Residential Mortgage Loans, following an increase in Canadian regulatory bank capital requirements.

Therefore, regulators and policymakers should:

- *Maintain regulatory capital requirements targeting Corporate & Commercial Loans, Residential Mortgage Loans, and Consumer/Retail Loans at levels equivalent or lower to those of periods prior or during economic downturn*. Economic downturns are driven by unfavourable economic policies and conditions.
- Set *different levels of capital reserve* requirements for *Corporate & Commercial Loans, Residential Mortgage Loans, and Consumer/Retail Loans*. This will enable regulators and policymakers to

optimally target these *key parts of the lending portfolio* that require increases in capital reserve.

Fourthly, the results found that the level of credit portfolio allocation by Canadian banks to other Consumer/Retail Loans is not directly impacted by changes in Canadian regulatory bank capital requirements. The level of credit portfolio allocation by Canadian banks to other Consumer/Retail Loans is rather impacted by macroeconomic variables such as GDP Gap, Business Climate, and Credit-to-GDP Gap.

This result found that, following 1% increases in GDP Gap, and Credit-to-GDP Gap, Canadian banks increased their level of credit portfolio allocation to Consumer/Retail Loans by 3.69% and 1.07% respectively, following 1% increases in Canadian regulatory bank capital requirements.

Additionally, the results found that even with improvements in business climate by 1%, the level of credit portfolio allocated to Consumer/Retail Loans, decreased by 4.36%, following increases in Canadian regulatory bank capital requirements (1%). This suggests that improvements in business climate are not sufficient to reduce the indirect impact of increases in regulatory capital requirements on Consumer/Retail Loans.

These results suggest that increases (favourable) in GDP Gap play an *alleviating role* on the indirect effect of increases in regulatory capital requirements on the level of Consumer/Retail Loans to the non-financial sector. However, increases (unfavourable) in Credit-to-GDP Gap do not worsen the indirect impact of increases in regulatory capital requirements on Consumer/Retail Loans.

Therefore, in addition to the fulfilment of the combination of the four favourable economic policy factors mentioned above (relevant for Corporate & Commercial Loans); regulators and policymakers should increase regulatory capital requirements on Consumer/Retail Loans prior or post-economic downturns when the economy registered increasing (favourable) GDP Gaps. In summary, regulators and policymakers should:

- *Only increase regulatory capital* requirements on Consumer/Retail Loans prior or post-economic downturns when a *combination* of the following *five favourable economic policy factors* is fulfilled:
  - (i) Increasing (favourable) GDP Gaps (specific to Consumer/Retail Loans),
  - (ii) Full employment (common with Corporate & Commercial Loans),

(iii) Economic expansion and growth (common with Corporate & Commercial Loans),
(iv) Price stability (common with Corporate & Commercial Loans),
(v) Expansionary fiscal policy (common with Corporate & Commercial Loans).

Overall, our results provide regulators and policymakers with empirical evidence suggesting the need to require different levels of capital requirements, targeting each of the following components of the portfolio of Canadian banks' loan to the non-financial sector: Corporate & Commercial Loans, Residential Mortgage Loans, and Consumer/Retail Loans.

Additionally, our studies provide regulators and policymakers with a combination of key economic factors necessary to ensure increases in regulatory capital requirements on Corporate & Commercial Loans, Residential Mortgage Loans, and Consumer/Retail Loans do not lead to tighter liquidity to the non-financial sector, which could negatively impact recovery efforts from an economic downturn.

Finally, our findings are in alignment with the results of previous studies such as Aiyar et al. (2016), Gropp et al. (2019), De Jonghe et al. (2020), and Imbierowicz et al. (2021), and contribute to the scarce literature regarding the impact of regulatory capital requirements on the lending volume of Canadian banks.

4.5 Robustness Tests

We performed a series of robustness checks to evaluate for the sensitivity of our results to changes in variables, model composition, and sample. Firstly, we re-estimated the regression model, excluding bank control variables.

Table 4.12 presents the results of the robustness check, evaluating the effect of changes in regulatory capital requirements on the three largest components of the portfolio of loan offered by Canadian banks to the non-financial sector, excluding bank control variables.

The results (Table 4.12) of the robustness check evaluating the effect of changes in regulatory capital requirements on the three largest components of the portfolio of loan offered by Canadian banks to the non-financial sector, excluding bank control variables, align with those previously obtained through the initial estimation of the multiple regression model (Model 3, Table 4.5).

Table 4.12 Impact of changes in bank regulatory capital requirements on Canadian banks' loan portfolio, excluding bank control variables

	Annual Δ Corp. & Commercial Loans	*Annual Δ Residential Mortgage Loans*	*Annual Δ Other Consumer/Retail Loans*
Independent Variables			
Annual Δ Canadian Bank Capital Requirements	**−0.44** **(0.02)****	**−0.33** **(0.03)****	0.10 (0.58)
Bank Control Variables			
Lagged (t−1) Return on Assets	Excluded	Excluded	Excluded
Lagged (t−1) Excess Capital	Excluded	Excluded	Excluded
Lagged (t−1) Ratio of Liquid Assets to Total Assets	Excluded	Excluded	Excluded
Lagged (t−1) Bank Size	Excluded	Excluded	Excluded
Lagged (t−1) Ratio of Core Deposit	Excluded	Excluded	Excluded
Macro. Control Variables			
Economic Policy	**−0.09** **(0.05)****	**−0.09** **(0.03)****	−0.04 (0.41)
GDP Gap	−0.99 (0.49)	−1.17 (0.37)	**3.75** **(0.02)****
Business Climate	1.72 (0.41)	−0.53 (0.77)	**−4.23** **(0.07)***
Credit-to-GDP Gap	0.31 (0.50)	0.27 (0.52)	**1.01** **(0.06)***
Other Details			
R^2	0.1386	0.0575	0.0283
Number of banks	120	120	120
Observations	153	191	212

Note: The statistical significance of results is indicated by *10% level, **5% level and ***1% level using standard errors. *p* values are presented in parentheses after coefficient estimates.

Secondly, we re-estimated the regression model, excluding macroeconomic control variables. Table 4.13 presents the results of the robustness check, evaluating the effect of changes in regulatory capital requirements on the three largest components of the portfolio of loan offered by Canadian banks to the non-financial sector, excluding macroeconomic control variables.

The results (Table 4.13) of the robustness check evaluating the effect of changes in regulatory capital requirements on the three largest components of the portfolio of loan offered by Canadian banks to the non-financial sector, excluding macroeconomic control variables, align with those

Table 4.13 Impact of changes in bank regulatory capital requirements on Canadian banks' loan portfolio, excluding macroeconomic control variables

	Annual Δ Corp. & Commercial Loans	*Annual Δ Residential Mortgage Loans*	*Annual Δ Other Consumer/ Retail Loans*
Independent Variables			
Annual Δ Canadian Bank Capital Requirements	**−0.48** **(0.01)*****	−0.24 (0.12)	0.12 (0.53)
Bank Control Variables			
Lagged (t−1) Return on Assets	−0.36 (0.94)	**−8.71** **(0.02)****	5.33 (0.25)
Lagged (t−1) Excess Capital	−0.003 (0.99)	0.19 (0.35)	−0.04 (0.87)
Lagged (t−1) Ratio of Liquid Assets to Total Assets	0.11 (0.49)	0.07 (0.56)	0.03 (0.81)
Lagged (t−1) Bank Size	4.17 (0.11)	-2.03 (0.39)	1.21 (0.68)
Lagged (t−1) Ratio of Core Deposit	**0.25** **(0.05)****	−0.03 (0.71)	0.14 (0.24)
Macro. Control Variables			
Economic Policy	Excluded	Excluded	Excluded
GDP Gap	Excluded	Excluded	Excluded
Business Climate	Excluded	Excluded	Excluded
Credit-to-GDP Gap	Excluded	Excluded	Excluded
Other Details			
R^2	0.0883	0.0927	0.0168
Number of banks	120	120	120
Observations	153	191	212

Note: The statistical significance of results is indicated by *10% level, **5% level and ***1% level using standard errors. *p* values are presented in parentheses after coefficient estimates.

previously obtained through the initial estimation of the multiple regression model (Model 3, Table 4.5).

Thirdly, we re-estimated the regression model, excluding bank and macroeconomic control variables. Table 4.14 presents the results of the robustness check, evaluating the effect of changes in regulatory capital requirements on the three main components of the portfolio of loan offered by Canadian banks to the non-financial sector, excluding bank control effects, and macroeconomic control variables.

The results (Table 4.14) of the robustness check evaluating the effect of changes in regulatory capital requirements on the three largest components of the portfolio of loan offered by Canadian banks to the

Table 4.14 Impact of changes in bank regulatory capital requirements on Canadian banks' loan portfolio, excluding bank and macroeconomic control variables

	Annual Δ Corp. & Commercial Loans	*Annual Δ Residential Mortgage Loans*	*Annual Δ Other Consumer/ Retail Loans*
Independent Variables			
Annual Δ Canadian Bank Capital Requirements	**–0.49** **(0.01)*****	**–0.30** **(0.05)****	0.13 (0.48)
Bank Control Variables			
Lagged (t–1) Return on Assets	Excluded	Excluded	Excluded
Lagged (t–1) Excess Capital	Excluded	Excluded	Excluded
Lagged (t–1) Ratio of Liquid Assets to Total Assets	Excluded	Excluded	Excluded
Lagged (t–1) Bank Size	Excluded	Excluded	Excluded
Lagged (t–1) Ratio of Core Deposit	Excluded	Excluded	Excluded
Macro. Control Variables			
Economic Policy	Excluded	Excluded	Excluded
GDP Gap	Excluded	Excluded	Excluded
Business Climate	Excluded	Excluded	Excluded
Credit-to-GDP Gap	Excluded	Excluded	Excluded
Other Details			
R^2	0.0374	0.0191	0.0023
Number of banks	120	120	120
Observations	153	191	212

Note: The statistical significance of results is indicated by *10% level, **5% level and ***1% level using standard errors. *p* values are presented in parentheses after coefficient estimates.

non-financial sector, excluding bank control variables and macroeconomic control variables, align with those previously obtained through the initial estimation of the multiple regression model (Model 3, Table 4.5).

4.6 Conclusion and Managerial Recommendation

This study investigated the effect of changes in regulatory capital requirements on the components of the portfolio of loan offered by Canadian banks to the non-financial sector. Our studies focused on the three largest components of the portfolio of loan offered by Canadian banks to the non-financial sector: Corporate & Commercial Loans (26% of Gross Loan), Residential Mortgage Loans (44% of Gross Loan), and Other Consumer/Retail Loans (20% of Gross Loan).

Firstly, our results found that a 1% increase in Canadian regulatory bank capital requirement ratio led to a decrease in Corporate & Commercial Loans by 0.44%. The results supporting the decrease in Corporate & Commercial Loans, following a 1% increase in Canadian regulatory bank capital requirement ratio are statistically significant. These results confirm that hypotheses H1 and H2 were rejected, in favour of hypothesis H0.

On the other hand, our results did not lead to statistically significant changes in Residential Mortgage Loans and Other Consumer/Retail Loans, following a 1% increase in Canadian regulatory bank capital requirement ratio. The results suggest that changes in Canadian regulatory bank capital requirement ratio had a direct downward impact on only the portion of the Canadian lending portfolio that accounts for Corporate & Commercial Loans. These results confirm that hypotheses H0 and H1 were rejected, in favour of hypothesis H2.

Secondly, the results found that the impact of the increase (1%) in the Canadian regulatory bank capital requirements on Corporate & Commercial Loans (–0.44%) is not dependent on changes in bank and macroeconomic control variables, except for Economic Policy. The results indicate that the impact of the increase in the Canadian regulatory bank capital requirements on Corporate & Commercial Loans is dependent on changes in economic policy uncertainty.

Thirdly, the results indicate that increases (1%) in the bank's Return on Asset over the previous year, and economic policy uncertainty, led to decreases in Residential Mortgage Loans by 7.95% and 0.08% respectively, following the increase of Canadian regulatory bank capital requirements. These results suggest that in times of economic policy uncertainty, Canadian banks with an increased level of return on asset over the previous year opted to decrease the level of their credit allocation towards Residential Mortgage Loans, following an increase in Canadian regulatory bank capital requirements.

Fourthly, the results found that the level of credit portfolio allocation by Canadian banks to other Consumer/Retail Loans is not directly impacted by changes in Canadian regulatory bank capital requirements. The level of credit portfolio allocation by Canadian banks to other Consumer/Retail Loans is rather impacted by macroeconomic variables such as GDP Gap, Business Climate, and Credit-to-GDP Gap.

Additionally, our results provide regulators and policymakers with empirical evidence suggesting the need to apply different levels of capital requirements targeting each of the components of the portfolio of Canadian banks' loan to the non-financial sector, separately.

Our studies also provide regulators and policymakers with a combination of key economic factors necessary to ensure that increases in regulatory capital requirements on Corporate & Commercial Loans, Residential Mortgage Loans, and Consumer/Retail Loans do not lead to tighter liquidity to the non-financial sector, which could negatively impact recovery efforts from an economic downturn. The Appendix provides a detailed summary of the managerial recommendations.

Our studies were limited by the existence of missed values and a sample that only covered the period post-subprime crisis (2012 to 2021). Theoretically, we have 1,200 observations (120 Canadian banks observed over 10 years). However, STATA only counts the number of observations for which there are values for all variables and years. Other limitations related to the presence of spurious outliers were mitigated by winsorising the samples utilised for the study of the research question.

Overall, our results are in alignment with the results of previous research studies such as Aiyar et al. (2016), Gropp et al. (2019), De Jonghe et al. (2020), and Imbierowicz et al. (2021) that contributed to the scarce literature on the impact of regulatory capital requirements on the lending behaviour of Canadian banks.

Chapter 5 presents a general conclusion on the analysis and findings presented in this book.

CHAPTER 5

General Conclusions

Abstract This book studied the impact of a microprudential and macroprudential regulation on the behaviour of financial institutions. Specifically, the empirical studies focused on the impact of changes in regulatory capital requirements on the lending behaviour of Canadian banks.

Overall, the results of the empirical studies contribute to the existing and scarce literature on regulatory capital requirements. They provide Canadian regulators and policymakers with guidelines and conditions necessary for the increase of the level of regulatory bank capital requirements, without negatively impacting the level of liquidity required to enable economic recovery from periods of economic uncertainty and downturns.

Keywords Basel Accords • Regulatory Capital Requirements • Macroprudential Regulations • Microprudential Regulations • GDP • Bank Size • Bank Liquidity • Monetary Policy • Inflation Rate (CPI) • GDP Gap • Business Climate • and Credit-to-GDP Gap • Canadian Bank Lending Behaviour • Canadian Bank Lending Portfolio • Canadian Bank Lending Volume • Canadian Bank Lending Interest

This book investigated the impact of changes in regulatory capital requirements on the lending behaviour of Canadian banks. Chapter 1 offered a general introduction.

B. Piper, *The Effect of Changes in Regulatory Capital Requirements on Banks Lending*
https://doi.org/10.1007/978-3-032-02208-0_5

Chapter 2 investigated the impact of banks' regulatory capital requirements on the lending volume of Canadian banks. In this chapter we studied the impact of banks' regulatory capital requirements on the Lending Volume of Canadian banks, by estimating a multiple regression model. The model, primarily, focused on the effect of regulatory capital levels on the volume of credit facilities offered by Canadian banks. Additionally, the model considered bank-specific determinants, as well as the macroeconomic environment in Canada. The industry-specific determinants allowed us to analyse the effect of the banking environment on the lending behaviour of Canadian banks. Similarly, the inclusion of the macroeconomic environment in our analysis enabled us to account for the macroeconomic effect on the credit allocation decisions of Canadian banks.

Our results contributed to the literature by showing that increases in Canadian regulatory bank capital requirement ratio led to a decrease in the volume gross loans offered by Canadian banks to the non-financial sector. Our results also demonstrated that regulators and policymakers can soften the effect of changes in regulatory capital requirements over the level of gross loans offered by Canadian to the non-financial sector, by increasing capital requirements only when a combination of specific favourable economic conditions is met.

Chapter 3 studied the impact of banks' regulatory capital requirements on the loan interest rate offered by Canadian banks. In this chapter, we investigated the impact of banks' regulatory capital requirements on the Loan Interest Rate offered by Canadian banks, by estimating the multiple regression model. The model, mainly, assessed on the effect of regulatory capital levels on the interest rate charged by Canadian banks for their offer of credit facilities. Furthermore, the model incorporated bank-specific determinants, as well as the macroeconomic environment in Canada. The industry-specific determinants allowed us to analyse the effect of the banking environment on the interest rate decisions by Canadian banks. Additionally, the incorporation of the macroeconomic environment in the study allowed us to account for the macroeconomic impact on the interest rate decisions of Canadian banks.

The results of Chapter 3 contributed to the literature by confirming that increases in regulatory capital requirements did not impact loan interest rates during normal economic times, characterised with economic growth and expansion. The findings are in line with those of Brei and Moreno (2019). Additionally, our study found that the impact of regulatory capital requirements on bank lending rate is indirectly controlled by Canadian banks' levels of liquidity and size.

Furthermore, the results of our analysis in Chapter 3 led to three recommendations to regulators and policymakers:

- Design and implement additional microprudential and supervisory tools to detect and impede the use a profit margin-boosting mechanism by Canadian banks, as the main avenue for complying with regulatory capital requirements. A profit margin-boosting mechanism consists of increasing loan interest rates to meet regulatory liquidity reserve requirements.
- Impose on banks the use of capital base increases, reduction of bank balance sheet risk, and sales of bank assets as tools to meet capital reserve requirements. This will ensure bank capital reserves are adequately diversified and resilient, leading to a more resilient banking industry.
- Maintain the CET1 surcharge of 1% of RWAs imposed by the OSFI on banks that are classified as D-SIBs to incorporate the additional risk derived from the size of these banks.

Chapter 4 investigated the impact of regulatory capital requirements on the Gross Loan Portfolio of Canadian banks. In this chapter we studied the impact of regulatory capital requirements on the Gross Loan Portfolio of Canadian banks by estimating three multiple regression models. The model primarily studied the effect of regulatory capital levels on the volume of the three main categories of credit facilities offered by Canadian banks. The three main categories of credit facilities are corporate and commercial loans, residential mortgage loans, and other consumer or retail loans. Additionally, the model considered bank-specific determinants as well as the macroeconomic environment in Canada.

The industry-specific determinants allowed us to analyse the effect of the banking environment on the behaviour of Canadian banks for each of the three categories of credit facilities. Similarly, the inclusion of the macroeconomic environment in our analysis enabled us to account for the macroeconomic effect on the behaviour of Canadian banks for each of the three categories of credit.

The results of our studies in Chapter 4 demonstrated that the changes in Canadian regulatory capital requirement ratio had a direct downward effect on only the portion of Canadian gross loan portfolio that represents Corporate & Commercial Loans. The effect of Canadian regulatory capital requirement on Corporate & Commercial Loans is not dependent on bank and macroeconomic control variables, except for economic policy.

Additionally, our studies in Chapter 4 found that in times of economic policy uncertainty, Canadian banks with an increased level of return on asset, over the previous year, were likely to decrease the volume of their gross loan's portfolio allocation towards Residential Mortgage Loans, following an increase in Canadian regulatory bank capital requirements.

Furthermore, our studies in Chapter 4 demonstrated that the volume of gross loan's portfolio allocation by Canadian banks to other Consumer/ Retail Loans is rather impacted by macroeconomic variables such as GDP Gap, Business Climate, and Credit-to-GDP Gap.

Finally, the results of our studies in Chapter 4 yielded additional recommendations to regulators and policymakers and provided further specifications on some of the recommendations that emanated from the results of the analysis conducted in Chapter 2. The Appendix provides a detailed summary of the managerial recommendations.

Future research avenues could cover the impact of regulatory capital requirements of interbank lending, cross-border capital flows, as well as the interactions between regulatory capital requirements and monetary policy, within the Canadian context. Future research could also cover the impact of regulatory capital requirements on Canadian banks' performance and GDP growth.

Appendix: Detailed Summary of Managerial Recommendations

B. Piper, *The Effect of Changes in Regulatory Capital Requirements on Banks Lending*
https://doi.org/10.1007/978-3-032-02208-0_6

Research Question	*Key Results*	*Managerial Recommendations* *Priority Level: High* *Target Institutions:* *1. The Superintendent of Financial Institutions (OSFI) &* *2. The Financial Sector Policy unit of the Department of Finance Canada*	*Academic & Managerial Impact*
What is the impact of banks' regulatory capital requirements on the Lending Volume of Canadian banks?	▪ Increases in Canadian regulatory bank capital requirement ratio led to a decrease in the volume of credit offered by Canadian banks to the non-financial sector, over the current year, considering macroeconomic control variables. ▪ The negative impact of tighter Canadian regulatory capital requirements on Canadian banks' lending volume to the non-financial sector can be soften by the fulfilment of a combination of the following four favourable economic policy factors: (i) Full employment (ii) Economic expansion and growth (iii) Price stability through the application of monetary policy tools (iv) Expansionary fiscal policy.	▪ During times of economic downturn, Canadian regulators and policymakers should maintain Canadian regulatory capital requirements at levels equivalent or lower to those of prior to the economic downturn period. ▪ Regulators and policymakers should only tighten regulatory capital requirements prior or post-economic downturns, when the following four conditions are met: (i) Full employment (ii) Economic expansion and growth (iii) Price stability through the application of monetary policy tools (iv) Expansionary fiscal policy.	▪ Provision of policy tools to mitigate liquidity shocks during times of economic downturn to ensure economic recovery is not halted (Managerial Impact). ▪ Contribution to the scarce literature on the impact of banks' regulatory capital requirements on the lending volume of Canadian banks. (Academic Impact).

Research Question	*Key Results*	*Managerial Recommendations* *Priority Level: High* *Target Institutions:* *1. The Superintendent of Financial Institutions (OSFI) &* *2. The Financial Sector Policy unit of the Department of Finance Canada*	*Academic & Managerial Impact*
What is the impact of banks' regulatory capital requirements on the Lending Rates of Canadian banks?	▪ Increases in regulatory capital requirements did not impact loan interest rates during normal economic times, characterised with economic growth and expansion. ▪ Canadian banks obtain increased return on assets by boosting their profit margin through increases in loan interest rates, following increases in regulatory capital requirements. ▪ Canadian banks with increasing levels of liquidity and bank size (assets) are more likely to maintain or decrease the level of their interest rates on loans offered to the non-financial sector, following increases in regulatory capital requirements. This suggests that the impact of regulatory capital requirements on bank lending rate is indirectly controlled by Canadian banks' levels of liquidity and size.	▪ While regulators and policymakers should increase bank capital requirements during normal economic times to ensure Canadian banks have adequate reserves, they should also use increases in regulatory capital requirements as a key policy tool during times of large capital inflows to deal with asset depreciation and other macroeconomic issues caused by the expansion of aggregate demand and inflationary pressure. ▪ Regulators and policy akers should design and implement additional microprudential and supervisory tools aimed at ensuring that banks do not use a profit margin-boosting mechanism, consisting of increasing loan interest rates, as the main avenue for meeting regulatory capital requirements.	▪ Provision of policy tools aimed at ensuring that increases in regulatory capital requirements do not lead to severe increases in lending interest rates on loans to the non-financial sector. (Managerial Impact). ▪ Provision of policy tools aimed at ensuring that bank capital reserves are adequately diversified and resilient, leading to a more resilient banking industry. (Managerial Impact).

Research Question	*Key Results*	*Managerial Recommendations* *Priority Level: High* *Target Institutions:* *1. The Superintendent of Financial Institutions (OSFI) &* *2. The Financial Sector Policy unit of the Department of Finance Canada*	*Academic & Managerial Impact*
		▪ Regulators and policymakers should require that banks build their capital reserve requirements using a combination of capital base increases, reduction of bank balance sheet risk, and sales of bank assets. ▪ Bank regulators and policymakers should ensure that banks with high levels of liquidity and size build additional reserves in the form of risk-based surcharges. The OSFI requires banks that are designated as D-SIBs to maintain a CET1 surcharge of 1% of RWAs. In alignment with our results, we recommend that OSFI keeps these measures to ensure that large banks maintain additional reserves to account for the supplementary risk engendered by their size.	▪ Contribution to the scarce literature on the impact of banks' regulatory capital requirements on the lending rates of Canadian banks. (Academic Impact).

Research Question	*Key Results*	*Managerial Recommendations* *Priority Level: High* *Target Institutions:* *1. The Superintendent of Financial Institutions (OSFI) &* *2. The Financial Sector Policy unit of the Department of Finance Canada*	*Academic & Managerial Impact*
What is the impact of banks' regulatory capital requirements on Canadian banks' Gross Loan Portfolio?	▪ A 1% increase in Canadian regulatory bank capital requirement ratio led to a decrease in Corporate & Commercial Loans by 0.44%. ▪ Changes in Canadian regulatory bank capital requirement ratio had a direct downward impact on only the portion of the Canadian lending portfolio that accounts for Corporate & Commercial Loans. ▪ The impact of the increase (1%) in the Canadian regulatory bank capital requirements on Corporate & Commercial Loans (–0.44%) is not dependent on changes in bank and macroeconomic control variables, except for Economic Policy. The results indicate that the impact of the increase in the Canadian regulatory bank capital requirements on Corporate & Commercial Loans is dependent on changes in Economic Policy uncertainty.	▪ Design and implement forecasting methodologies that enable the determination of the *optimal level* of Canadian regulatory bank capital requirements on Corporate & Commercial Loans. The imposition of Canadian regulatory bank capital requirements on Corporate & Commercial Loans beyond its optimal level can lead to sharp decreases in liquidity and credit allocation towards the non-financial Corporate & Commercial sector. ▪ *Only increase regulatory capital* requirements on Corporate & Commercial Loans prior or post-economic downturns when a *combination* of the following *four favourable economic policy factors* is fulfilled: (i) Full employment (ii) Economic expansion and growth	▪ Provision of policy tools to mitigate liquidity shocks during times of economic downturn to ensure economic recovery is not halted (Managerial Impact). ▪ Contribution to the scarce literature on the impact of banks' regulatory capital requirements on the lending volume of Canadian banks. (Academic Impact).

Research Question	*Key Results*	*Managerial Recommendations* *Priority Level: High* *Target Institutions:* *1. The Superintendent of Financial Institutions (OSFI) &* *2. The Financial Sector Policy unit of the Department of Finance Canada*	*Academic & Managerial Impact*
		(iii) Price stability through the application of monetary policy tools (iv) Expansionary fiscal policy. ▪ Regulators and policymakers should *maintain regulatory capital* requirements *targeting* Corporate & Commercial Loans, Residential Mortgage Loans, and Consumer/Retail Loans *at levels equivalent or lower* to those of periods prior or during economic downturn. Economic downturns are driven by unfavourable economic policies and conditions.	

Research Question	*Key Results*	*Managerial Recommendations* *Priority Level: High* *Target Institutions:* ***1. The Superintendent of Financial Institutions (OSFI) &*** ***2. The Financial Sector Policy unit of the Department of Finance Canada***	*Academic & Managerial Impact*
What is the impact of banks' regulatory capital requirements on Canadian banks' Gross Loan Portfolio?	▪ Increases (1%) in the bank's Return on Asset over the previous year, and Economic Policy uncertainty, led to decreases in Residential Mortgage Loans by 7.95% and 0.08% respectively, following the increase of Canadian regulatory bank capital requirements. These results suggest that in times of Economic Policy uncertainty, Canadian banks with an increased level of return on asset over the previous year opted to decrease the level of their credit allocation towards Residential Mortgage Loans, following an increase in Canadian regulatory bank capital requirements. ▪ The level of credit portfolio allocation by Canadian banks to other Consumer/Retail Loans is not directly impacted by changes in Canadian regulatory bank capital requirements. The level of credit portfolio allocation by Canadian banks to other Consumer/Retail Loans is rather impacted by macroeconomic variables such as GDP Gap, Business Climate, and Credit-to-GDP Gap.	▪ Regulators and policymakers should set *different levels of capital reserve* requirements for Corporate & Commercial Loans, Residential Mortgage Loans, and Consumer/Retail Loans. This will enable regulators and policymakers to *optimally target* these *key parts of the lending portfolio* that require increases in capital reserve.	▪ Provision of policy tools to mitigate liquidity shocks during times of economic downturn to ensure economic recovery is not halted (Managerial Impact). ▪ Contribution to the scarce literature on the impact of banks' regulatory capital requirements on the lending volume of Canadian banks. (Academic Impact).

Bibliography

Abbas, F., Iqbal, S., & Aziz, B. (2020). The role of bank liquidity and bank risk in determining bank capital: Empirical analysis of Asian banking industry. *Review of Pacific Basin Financial Markets & Policies, 23*(3), 1–21. https://doi.org/10.1142/S0219091520500175

Abbas, F., Iqbal, S., Aziz, B., & Yang, Z. (2019). The impact of bank capital, bank liquidity and credit risk on profitability in postcrisis period: A comparative study of US and Asia. *Cogent Economics & Finance, 7*(1), 1–10. https://doi.org/10.1080/23322039.2019.1605683

Acharya, V. V., Imbierowicz, B., Steffen, S., & Teichmann, D. (2020). Does the lack of financial stability impair the transmission of monetary policy? *Journal of Financial Economics, 138*(2), 342–365. https://doi.org/10.1016/j.jfineco.2020.04.004

Aiyar, S., Calomiris, C. W., & Wieladek, T. (2016). How does credit supply respond to monetary policy and bank minimum capital requirements? *European Economic Review, 82*, 142–165. https://doi.org/10.1016/j.euroecorev.2015.07.021

Bahaj, S., & Malherbe, F. (2020). The forced safety effect: How higher capital requirements can increase bank lending. *Journal of Finance, 75*(6), 3013–3057. https://doi.org/10.1111/jofi.12917

Bank of Canada. (2022, July). *Product market: Definitions, graphs and data. Estimates of the output gap.* https://www.bankofcanada.ca/?p=39818

Bank of Canada. (2022, July). *Business outlook survey data.* https://www.bankofcanada.ca/publications/bos/business-outlook-survey-data/

Bank for International Settlements. (2022, July). *Credit-to-GDP trend (HP filter).* https://stats.bis.org/statx/srs/table/f2.1?p=20174&c=

B. Piper, *The Effect of Changes in Regulatory Capital Requirements on Banks Lending*
https://doi.org/10.1007/978-3-032-02208-0_6

Bank for International Settlements. (2023, August). *History of the Basel Committee.* https://www.bis.org/bcbs/history.htm

Bank for International Settlements. (2023, August). *International convergence of capital measurement and capital standards.* https://www.bis.org/publ/bcbs04a.pdf

Bank for International Settlements. (2023, August). *Basel II: International convergence of capital measurement and capital standards.* https://www.bis.org/publ/bcbs118.pdf

Bank for International Settlements. (2023, August). *Basel III: Responding to the 2007–09 financial crisis.* https://www.bis.org/bcbs/history.htm

Bank for International Settlements. (2023, August). *Minimum risk-based capital requirements.* https://www.bis.org/basel_framework/chapter/RBC/20.htm

Bank for International Settlements. (2023, August). *The capital buffers in Basel III – Executive summary.* https://www.bis.org/fsi/fsisummaries/b3_capital.htm

Barth, A., & Mansouri, S. (2021). Corporate culture and banking. *Journal of Economic Behavior & Organization, 186*, 46–75. https://doi.org/10.1016/j.jebo.2021.03.022

Begenau, J. (2020). Capital requirements, risk choice, and liquidity provision in a business-cycle model. *Journal of Financial Economics, 136*(2), 355–378. https://doi.org/10.1016/j.jfineco.2019.09.006

Behn, M., Haselmann, R., & Wachtel, P. (2016). Procyclical capital regulation and lending. *Journal of Finance, 71*(2), 919–956. https://doi.org/10.1111/jofi.12383

Ben Naceur, S., Marton, K., & Roulet, C. (2018). Basel III, and bank-lending: Evidence from the United States and Europe. *Journal of Financial Stability, 39*, 1–27. https://doi.org/10.1016/j.jfs.2018.08.001

Benetton, M., Eckley, P., Garbarino, N., Kirwin, L., & Latsi, G. (2021). Capital requirements and mortgage pricing: Evidence from Basel II. *Journal of Financial Intermediation, 48*, 100883. https://doi.org/10.1016/j.jfi.2020.100883

Bichsel, R., Lambertini, L., Mukherjee, A., & Wunderli, D. (2021). The pass-through of bank capital requirements to corporate lending spreads. *Journal of Financial Stability, 57*, 100910. https://doi.org/10.1016/j.jfs.2021.100910

Bolton, P., Freixas, X., Gambacorta, L., & Mistrulli, P. E. (2016). Relationship and transaction lending in a crisis. *Review of Financial Studies, 29*(10), 2643–2676. https://doi.org/10.1093/rfs/hhw041

Brei, M., & Moreno, R. (2019). Reserve requirements and capital flows in Latin America. *Journal of International Money & Finance, 99*, 102079. https://doi.org/10.1016/j.jimonfin.2019.102079

Brigida, M. (2019). The effect of bank regulatory capital levels on loan types. *Banking & Finance Review, 11*(2), 91–117. https://ssrn.com/abstract=3372705

Broll, U., Welzel, P., & Wong, K. P. (2018). Ambiguity preferences, risk taking and the banking firm. *Eurasian Economic Review, 8*(3), 343–353. https://doi.org/10.1007/s40822-018-0101-1

Bui, C., Scheule, H., & Wu, E. (2017). The value of bank capital buffers in maintaining financial system resilience. *Journal of Financial Stability*, *33*, 23–40. https://doi.org/10.1016/j.jfs.2017.11.004

Campbell, J., Lo, A., & MacKinlay, A. (1996). *The econometrics of financial markets* (629 pp.). Princeton University Press.

Casu, B., Di Pietro, F., & Trujillo-Ponce, A. (2019). Liquidity creation and bank capital. *Journal of Financial Services Research*, *56*(3), 307–340. https://doi.org/10.1007/s10693-018-0293-2

Chevalier, F., Cloutier, M., & Mitev, N. (2019). *Research methods for the DBA* (548 pp.). Business Science Institute Collection.

Cohen, B. H., & Scatigna, M. (2016). Banks, and capital requirements: Channels of adjustment. *Journal of Banking & Finance*, *69*, S56–S69. https://doi.org/10.1016/j.jbankfin.2015.09.022

Cummings, J. R., & Durrani, K. J. (2016). Effect of the Basel Accord capital requirements on the loan-loss provisioning practices of Australian banks. *Journal of Banking & Finance*, *67*, 23–36. https://doi.org/10.1016/j.jbankfin.2016.02.006

De Jonghe, O., Dewachter, H., & Ongena, S. (2020). Bank capital (requirements) and credit supply: Evidence from pillar 2 decisions. *Journal of Corporate Finance*, *60*, 101518. https://doi.org/10.1016/j.jcorpfin.2019.101518

De Jonghe, O., Dewachter, H., Mulier, K., Ongena, S., & Schepens, G. (2020). Some borrowers are more equal than others: Bank funding shocks and credit reallocation. *Review of Finance*, *24*(1), 1–43. https://doi.org/10.1093/rof/rfz019

Degryse, H., Karapetyan, A., & Karmakar, S. (2021). To ask or not to ask? Bank capital requirements and loan collateralization. *Journal of Financial Economics*, *142*(1), 239–260. https://doi.org/10.1016/j.jfineco.2021.03.008

Deli, Y. D., & Hasan, I. (2017). Real effects of bank capital regulations: Global evidence. *Journal of Banking & Finance*, *82*, 217–228. https://doi.org/10.1016/j.jbankfin.2017.05.011

DeYoung, R., Distinguin, I., & Tarazi, A. (2018). The joint regulation of bank liquidity and bank capital. *Journal of Financial Intermediation*, *34*, 32–46. https://doi.org/10.1016/j.jfi.2017.12.004

Economic Policy Uncertainty Research Group. (2022, July). *News-based policy uncertainty index*. http://www.policyuncertainty.com

El-Massah, S., Bacheer, S. M., & Al Sayed, O. (2019). Liquidity risk in the MENA region banking sector: Does bank type make a difference? *Journal of Developing Areas*, *53*(1), 147–163. https://doi.org/10.1353/jda.2019.0010

Federal Reserve Bank of St. Louis. (2023, August). *Coping with bank failures: Some lessons from the United States and the United Kingdom*. https://files.stlouisfed.org/files/htdocs/publications/review/86/12/Coping_Dec1986.pdf

Federal Reserve History. (2023, August). *Savings and loan crisis*. https://www.federalreservehistory.org/essays/savings-and-loan-crisis

Financial Stability Board. (2023, August). *Principles on loss-absorbing and recapitalisation capacity of G-SIBs in resolution.* https://www.fsb.org/wp-content/uploads/TLAC-Principles-and-Term-Sheet-for-publication-final.pdf

Fitch Solutions. (2022, July). *Canadian bank financials data, from 2012 to 2021.* Fitch Solutions.

Gambacorta, L., & Murcia, A. (2020). The impact of macroprudential policies in Latin America: An empirical analysis using credit registry data. *Journal of Financial Intermediation*, *42*, 100828. https://doi.org/10.1016/j.jfi.2019.04.002

Gambacorta, L., & Shin, H. S. (2018). Why bank capital matters for monetary policy. *Journal of Financial Intermediation*, *35*, 17–29. https://doi.org/10.1016/j.jfi.2017.05.004

Glancy, D., & Kurtzman, R. (2018). How do capital requirements affect loan rates? Evidence from high volatility commercial real estate. *US Federal Reserve Board's Finance & Economic Discussion Series*, 2018(035), 1–42. https://doi.org/10.17016/FEDS.2018.035

Gopalakrishnan, B., Jacob, J., & Mohapatra, S. (2021). Risk-sensitive Basel regulations and firms' access to credit: Direct and indirect effects. *Journal of Banking & Finance*, *126*, 106101. https://doi.org/10.1016/j.jbankfin.2021.106101

Gourieroux, C., & Jasiak, J. (2018). *Financial econometrics: Problems, models, and methods* (529 pp.). Princeton University Press.

Gropp, R., Mosk, T., Ongena, S., & Wix, C. (2019). Banks' response to higher capital requirements: Evidence from a quasi-natural experiment. *Review of Financial Studies*, *32*(1), 266–299. https://doi.org/10.1093/rfs/hhy052

Igan, D., & Mirzaei, A. (2020). Does going tough on banks make the going gets tough? Bank liquidity regulations, capital requirements, and sectoral activity. *Journal of Economic Behavior & Organization*, *177*, 688–726. https://doi.org/10.1016/j.jebo.2020.06.018

Imbierowicz, B., Kragh, J., & Rangvid, J. (2018). Time-varying capital requirements and disclosure rules: Effects on capitalization and lending decisions. *Journal of Money, Credit & Banking*, *50*(4), 573–602. https://doi.org/10.1111/jmcb.12456

Imbierowicz, B., Löffler, A., & Vogel, U. (2021). The transmission of bank capital requirements and monetary policy to bank lending in Germany. *Review of International Economics*, *29*(1), 144–164. https://doi.org/10.1111/roie.12497

Jiménez, G., Ongena, S., Peydró, J.-L., & Saurina, J. (2017). Macroprudential policy, countercyclical bank capital buffers, and credit supply: Evidence from the Spanish dynamic provisioning experiments. *Journal of Political Economy*, *125*(6), 2126–2177. https://doi.org/10.1086/694289

Jordà, Ò., Richter, B., Schularick, M., & Taylor, A. M. (2021). Bank capital redux: Solvency, liquidity, and crisis. *Review of Economic Studies*, *88*(1), 260–286. https://doi.org/10.1093/restud/rdaa038

Juelsrud, R. E., & Wold, E. G. (2020). Risk-weighted capital requirements and portfolio rebalancing. *Journal of Financial Intermediation*, *41*, 100806. https://doi.org/10.1016/j.jfi.2019.03.001

Kanngiesser, D., Martin, R., Maurin, L., & Moccero, D. (2020). The macroeconomic impact of shocks to bank capital buffers in the Euro area. *The B.E. Journal of Macroeconomics*, *20*(1), 1–17. https://doi.org/10.1515/bejm-2018-0314

Klinac, I., Peša, A., & Bolfek, B. (2019). Influence of regulatory capital requirements on the self-financing capacity of a banking company. *Business and Economic Horizons*, *15*(1), 70–89. https://doi.org/10.15208/beh.2019.6

Komath, M. A. C., Doğan, M., & Sayılır, Ö. (2023). Impact of corporate governance and related controversies on the market value of banks. *Research in International Business and Finance*, *65*, 101985. https://doi.org/10.1016/j.ribaf.2023.101985

Laidroo, L. (2016). Bank ownership and lending: Does bank ownership matter? *Emerging Markets Finance & Trade*, *52*(2), 285–301. https://doi.org/10.1080/1540496X.2016.1116288

Lee, S. J., & Stebunovs, V. (2016). Bank capital pressures, loan substitutability, and nonfinancial employment. *Journal of Economics and Business*, *83*, 44–69. https://doi.org/10.1016/j.jeconbus.2015.12.004

Ly, K. C., & Shimizu, K. (2021). Did Basel regulation cause a significant procyclicality? *Journal of International Financial Markets, Institutions and Money*, *73*, 101365. https://doi.org/10.1016/j.intfin.2021.101365

Mankart, J., Michaelides, A., & Pagratis, S. (2020). Bank capital buffers in a dynamic model. *Financial Management*, *49*(2), 473–502. https://doi.org/10.1111/fima.12278

Meeks, R. (2017). Capital regulation and the macroeconomy: Empirical evidence and macroprudential policy. *European Economic Review*, *95*, 125–141. https://doi.org/10.1016/j.euroecorev.2017.03.010

Noss, J., & Toffano, P. (2016). Estimating the impact of changes in aggregate bank capital requirements on lending and growth during an upswing. *Journal of Banking & Finance*, *62*, 15–27. https://doi.org/10.1016/j.jbankfin.2015.10.003

Office of the Superintendent of Financial Institutions. (2022, July). *Requirements for inclusion in regulatory capital*. https://www.osfi-bsif.gc.ca/Eng/fi-if/rg-ro/gdn-ort/gl-ld/Pages/CAR18_chpt2.aspx

Office of the Superintendent of Financial Institutions. (2022, July). *Tier 2 capital*. https://www.osfi-bsif.gc.ca/Eng/fi-if/rg-ro/gdn-ort/gl-ld/Pages/CAR18_chpt2.aspx

Office of the Superintendent of Financial Institutions. (2022, July). *Calculation of OSFI minimum capital requirements*. https://www.osfi-bsif.gc.ca/Eng/fi-if/rg-ro/gdn-ort/gl-ld/Pages/CAR22_chpt1.aspx

Office of the Superintendent of Financial Institutions. (2022, July). *Overview of risk-based capital requirements*. https://www.osfi-bsif.gc.ca/Eng/fi-if/rg-ro/gdn-ort/gl-ld/Pages/CAR22_chpt1.aspx

Office of the Superintendent of Financial Institutions. (2022, July). *Overview of risk-based capital requirements – Scope of application*. https://www.osfi-bsif.gc.ca/Eng/fi-if/rg-ro/gdn-ort/gl-ld/Pages/CAR22_chpt1.aspx

Office of the Superintendent of Financial Institutions. (2022, July). *Overview of risk-based capital requirements – Total risk-weighted assets.* https://www.osfi-bsif.gc.ca/Eng/fi-if/rg-ro/gdn-ort/gl-ld/Pages/CAR22_chpt1.aspx

Office of the Superintendent of Financial Institutions. (2022, July). *Overview of risk-based capital requirements – Mandated capital buffers.* https://www.osfi-bsif.gc.ca/Eng/fi-if/rg-ro/gdn-ort/gl-ld/Pages/CAR22_chpt1.aspx

Office of the Superintendent of Financial Institutions. (2022, July). *Overview of risk-based capital requirements – Annex 2 supervisory target capital requirements.* https://www.osfi-bsif.gc.ca/Eng/fi-if/rg-ro/gdn-ort/gl-ld/Pages/CAR22_chpt1.aspx

Office of the Superintendent of Financial Institutions. (2022, November). *Domestic systemically important bank (D-SIB) surcharge.* https://www.osfi-bsif.gc.ca/Eng/fi-if/rg-ro/gdn-ort/gl-ld/Pages/CAR22_chpt1.aspx#ToC1.8

Office of the Superintendent of Financial Institutions. (2023, August). *Capital adequacy requirements (CAR) Chapter 1 – Overview.* https://www.osfi-bsif.gc.ca/Eng/fi-if/rg-ro/gdn-ort/gl-ld/Pages/CAR19_chpt1.aspx

Office of the Superintendent of Financial Institutions. (2023, August). *Our role.* https://www.osfi-bsif.gc.ca/Eng/osfi-bsif/Pages/default.aspx

Roulet, C. (2018). Basel III: Effects of capital and liquidity regulations on European bank lending. *Journal of Economics & Business, 95*, 26–46. https://doi.org/10.1016/j.jeconbus.2017.10.001

Single Resolution Board. (2023, August). *The minimum requirement for own funds and eligible liabilities (MREL).* https://www.srb.europa.eu/en/system/files?file=media/document/mrel_policy_may_2021_final_web.pdf#:~:text=The%20minimum%20requirement%20for%20own%20funds%20and%20eligible,facilitate%20the%20implementation%20of%20the%20preferred%20resolution%20strategy

International Monetary Fund. (2023, August). *Financial soundness indicators (FSIs).* https://data.imf.org/regular.aspx?key=63174546

World Bank. (2023, August). *GDP (current US$) – Canada.* https://data.worldbank.org/indicator/NY.GDP.MKTP.CD?locations=CA&most_recent_value_desc=true

Uluc, A., & Wieladek, T. (2018). Capital requirements, monetary policy and risk shifting in the mortgage market. *Journal of Financial Intermediation, 35*(Part B), 3–16. https://doi.org/10.1016/j.jfi.2016.09.004

Index

B. Piper, *The Effect of Changes in Regulatory Capital Requirements on Banks Lending*
https://doi.org/10.1007/978-3-032-02208-0_6

FSC
www.fsc.org
MIX
Papier | Fördert
gute Waldnutzung
FSC® C083411

Kolibri 360 GmbH
Ferdinand-Jühlke-Straße 7
99095 Erfurt, Deutschland
produktsicherheit@kolibri360.de